DATE			

THE

WOMEN'S RIGHTS
MOVEMENT

MOVING TOWARD EQUALITY

REFORM MOVEMENTS
IN AMERICAN
HISTORY

THE
WOMEN'S RIGHTS
MOVEMENT

MOVING TOWARD EQUALITY

Shane Mountjoy

Series Editor
Tim McNeese

CHELSEA HOUSE
PUBLISHERS
An imprint of Infobase Publishing

Cover: Four members of the National Woman's Party march in Washington, D.C., in support of women's suffrage in February 1917.

The Women's Rights Movement: Moving Toward Equality

Chelsea House
An imprint of Infobase Publishing
132 West 31st Street
New York NY 10001

Library of Congress Cataloging-in-Publication Data
Mountjoy, Shane, 1967–
  The Women's rights movement : moving toward equality / Shane Mountjoy.
      p. cm. — (Reform movements in American history)
  Includes bibliographical references and index.
  ISBN-13: 978-0-7910-9505-8 (hardcover)
  ISBN-10: 0-7910-9505-3 (hardcover)
  1. Women's rights—United States—History. I. Title. II. Series.

  HQ1236.5.U5M68 2007
  305.420973—dc22

                              2007021696

Chelsea House books are available at special discounts when purchased in bulk quantities for businesses, associations, institutions, or sales promotions. Please call our Special Sales Department in New York at (212) 967-8800 or (800) 322-8755.

You can find Chelsea House on the World Wide Web at http://www.chelseahouse.com

Series design by Kerry Casey
Cover design by Ben Peterson

Printed in the United States of America

Bang EJB 10 9 8 7 6 5 4 3 2 1

This book is printed on acid-free paper.

All links and Web addresses were checked and verified to be correct at the time of publication. Because of the dynamic nature of the Web, some addresses and links may have changed since publication and may no longer be valid.

CONTENTS

"Be a Good Boy"

The air was hot and humid on that mid-August afternoon in 1920. Dozens of people packed the Tennessee House chamber, in Nashville, to witness the historic vote. Nearly a week before, the Tennessee Senate had voted in favor of ratifying the Nineteenth Amendment, which would guarantee women's suffrage, or the right to vote. Albert H. Roberts, the governor of Tennessee, called a special session of the legislature to consider the proposed amendment. The Tennessee General Assembly had first convened on Monday, August 9, to deliberate the issue. One young member, Harry Burn from Niota, located in the mountains of eastern Tennessee, took his seat and participated in the proceedings. On that day, he was a relatively unknown member of the legislature. When the session ended a week and a half later, however, he was a virtual celebrity throughout the United States.

This special session in Tennessee was anything but ordinary. Thirty-five other states had already voted to ratify the Nineteenth Amendment, and to win ratification, supporters needed only one more state to give approval. Prior to the session in Tennessee, the chances of success appeared certain. Dignitaries, activists, reporters, and interested citizens sat, stood, and occupied any available space in order to watch the legislators in session. The smell of roses, red and yellow, filled the air. On their lapels, many of the members wore red roses, signaling their opposition to the amendment. Others displayed yellow roses, signifying their support for suffrage. Throughout the gallery, others also wore roses, some red, some yellow. This was indeed a special session of the Tennessee General Assembly.

There were other issues to consider, as well. The Tennessee state constitution specified that following the passage of an amendment to the U.S. Constitution by Congress, the state legislature could take no action on it until after the next election. Congress passed the Nineteenth Amendment in June 1919. Consequently, in the case of Tennessee, the next election was not to occur until the fall of 1920. Supreme Court rulings had already established federal supremacy in instances of conflict between the federal and a state constitution. Nevertheless, opponents of the amendment promised to fight ratification in Tennessee on the grounds the vote was in violation of the state constitution. Even if Tennessee voted to ratify, legal challenges were sure to follow.

Carrie Chapman Catt, president of the National American Woman Suffrage Association (NAWSA), had come to Tennessee a few weeks before to offer her support to the cause. Catt, a prominent suffragist, had fought for women's right to vote for nearly 30 years. In 1920, she was one of the most recognizable women in the suffrage movement. On her arrival, she immediately went on a speaking tour of the state to champion the cause of female suffrage. She spoke at rallies, large meetings, and campaign forums. Despite the hot weather, Catt did what she seemed to do best: She condensed the major issues into just two main points, both of which could be easily communicated. Catt argued that rulings by the U.S. Supreme Court closed the debate on any conflict between Tennessee's constitution and the U.S. Constitution. She also insisted that supporters of women's suffrage in Tennessee faced

FIFTEEN CENTS

TIME
The Weekly News-Magazine

Vol. VII, No. 24

AN IOWA FARMER'S DAUGHTER
Mrs. Carrie Chapman Catt
(See Page 8)

June 14, 1926

Pictured here on the cover of the June 14, 1926, issue of *Time*, Carrie Chapman Catt was one of the leading proponents of women's suffrage in the early twentieth century. She served two terms as the president of the National American Woman Suffrage Association (NAWSA) and played a prominent role in securing ratification of the Nineteenth Amendment.

opposition by large, wealthy interests from outside the state. Specifically, she identified a "sinister combination of the whiskey lobby, the manufacturers' lobby, and the railroad lobby."[1]

In the year 1920, a presidential election would also take place. Both the Republican candidate, Warren G. Harding, and the Democratic candidate, James M. Cox, conveyed their support in personal letters to Carrie Chapman Catt. In addition, the Republicans and Democrats sent the vice chairs of their parties as their representatives to be on hand for the voting in Tennessee. Finally, there were numerous state committees from both parties on hand. The National Woman's Party had a committee for supporting ratification. Even Governor Roberts had his own committee. There were many different groups, and although each one supported the same cause, they ran the risk of creating chaos. The committees met and decided to coordinate their efforts. This combined group selected the vice chair of the Democratic Party, Charl Williams, as their chair, to synchronize their actions. This general committee then made the decision that all lobbying in the Tennessee General Assembly was to be done by Tennessee women. By doing this, the suffragists lessened the chance of offending state politicians, many of whom might resent outside forces exerting pressure in the state legislature.

Opponents of women's suffrage also flocked to the state's capital. One national figure who favored the status quo was Everett P. Wheeler, head of the Men's Anti-Suffrage Association, only recently renamed the more politically acceptable American Constitutional League. He arrived in Nashville to lobby against ratification. Wheeler capably enlisted the aid of several prominent officials, who in turn expended every effort to change the vote of those favoring suffrage. These attempts proved to be extremely effective, as more and more supporters of ratification began to change their votes.

In the days and weeks leading up to the special session, legislators, activists, and many others converged on Nashville in anticipation of the political showdown. The special session of the Tennessee General Assembly commenced on Monday August 9, 1920. The topic of women's suffrage produced heated debate in each house. The state Senate, after just four days, voted to ratify the amendment by a vote of 24 to 4. All attention now focused on the House, where Seth Walker, the speaker, was a member of the women's ratification committee.

Antisuffrage efforts succeeded in convincing Walker to "become the leader of the opposition!"[2] As Speaker of the House, Walker used his power to postpone the vote in order to ensure rejection of the amendment. Before the session began, suffragists had confirmed support from 62 members of the House. Nonetheless, members began to retract their support, especially after Walker's defection. Soon, activists on both sides realized the final vote was going to be extremely close. As the session wore on and the impending vote loomed, supporters and opponents of the amendment redoubled their efforts to influence the vote. As the session continued, the pressure mounted. On Wednesday, August 18, the second week of speeches and motions finally culminated in the all-important vote. Despite the seemingly endless debate, the waiting was almost over.

THE HOUR HAS COME!

The battle in the House grew more intense. By all counts, the vote was too close to call. Finally, the speaker of the House, Seth Walker, ended all debate with the swinging of his gavel. Then he declared, "The hour has come! The battle has been fought and won!"[3] He then entered a motion that the resolution be tabled. Such a postponement would likely doom the chances of ratification in Tennessee. The chamber grew silent as the clerk began the roll-call vote. The house clerk slowly read the names of each member, and dutifully recorded the responses for and against the motion to table the measure. All was quiet until one member, Banks Turner, voted against tabling the resolution. Turner was originally an antisuffrage Democrat who was persuaded to support the suffragists. The chamber erupted for a few moments. Most present realized that the suffragists now had enough votes to call for a vote on the amendment. The roll call continued, but the motion to table the resolution failed to carry, ending in a tie vote, 48 to 48.

Speaker Walker was very aware of the impact of Turner's vote, and he was not too pleased with it. Walker called for another roll call to be taken. Then, the speaker went to Banks Turner's chair, "threw his arm around him and poured frenzied entreaties into his ear."[4] Walker remained there, with his arm around Turner throughout the vote. When the clerk finally called his name, Turner waited briefly before pushing Walker's arm off his shoulder and shouting his vote of "No." Again, the House ended with a 48–48 deadlock on the motion. Without question, the motion to table the resolution had failed to carry.

Now the vote on the amendment itself began. The two roll-call votes revealed the chamber was stalemated with equal numbers for and against the suffrage amendment. A tie on this vote would end any chance of ratification in Tennessee. Suffragists cringed as they considered this possible outcome.

For the third time that day, the clerk began a roll call to record each member's vote. Once again, Harry Burn waited nervously for the clerk to read his name. He cast his two previous votes that day to table the amendment. In effect, his two earlier votes were against suffrage. This was no surprise, as he wore a red rose on his lapel, indicating his opposition to the amendment. Suffragists viewed him as a "no" vote. The vote posed a great deal of tension for

Burn, however. Because he was the youngest member of the General Assembly at just 24 years of age, his vote was not deemed important. The roll call continued, and young Harry Burn restlessly waited.

At the time, no one else knew that Burn held in his pocket a note from his mother. In it, she discussed the upcoming suffrage vote and expressed an unfavorable view of suffrage opponents. As he sat waiting for his turn to vote, Burn thought about his mother and her letter. One particular phrase continued to weigh on his mind; his mother had written, "Don't forget to be a good boy" and vote for ratification.[5] The clerk called his name. Burn looked at the red rose on his lapel, but he thought of his mother and the note in his pocket. Harry hesitated and then called out his vote. Which way did he vote? Did he listen to his mother? What became of the proposed amendment to the Constitution?

Women's Rights Throughout History

How was it that women in the United States were unable to vote until 1920? The United States was founded on principles of political equality, yet female citizens lacked the basic political right of suffrage for nearly 150 years after the signing of the Declaration of Independence. Throughout history, women have been subjected to unequal treatment from legal codes within various societies and cultures. Many legal precedents that affected women at the time of the American Revolution can be traced to ancient times. The colonial and early American legal codes reflected the influence of English law, which in turn was influenced by ancient Roman law. These Roman practices provided insight into the legal codes that placed rigid restraints on women, even women in the United States.

WOMEN'S RIGHTS IN THE ROMAN WORLD

Under Roman law, women were entirely reliant upon their male relatives. When a woman married, her father's authority shifted to her husband, as she was then subject to "the power of her husband."[6] Women gained the right to make a will at the youthful age of 12, but that right was mitigated by the requirement that a male relative give his blessing to the will. Unmarried women remained under the permanent protection and guardianship of their father. Upon his death, the closest male relative assumed the powers of guardianship. In the event that there were not any close male relatives by birth, then the entire extended family assumed the responsibility of providing for the woman. Married women fared no better, as their property was under the control of their husbands.

One author summed up the plight of Roman women this way: "Throughout her life a woman was supposed to remain absolutely under the power of father, husband, or guardian, and to do nothing without their consent."[7] Male power in ancient times even allowed for, albeit in rare circumstances such as adultery, the father or husband to put the woman to death after consulting with the family. Women in such times faced a pitiable existence.

Lacking the legal right to obtain Roman citizenship left women exposed to certain punishments reserved for noncitizens, such as public floggings and crucifixion. In other situations, women were exempt from torture, simply because of their sex. Without citizenship, women had no right to appeal to the Roman emperor, or caesar, meaning women were bound by the rulings of lesser officials. Further, because Roman citizenship included rights and privileges throughout the empire, the denial of citizenship meant the denial of basic rights. The few legal protections offered to women stemmed from the presumption of feminine frailties. These exemptions included immunity from torture in most cases, the right to plead ignorance in civil cases, and inheritance rights in instances of no will.

Women could not hold public office or perform civic duties such as voting. Nor could a woman serve as a witness in court proceedings (except in cases of witchcraft or treason) enter into contracts. Roman law prohibited women from teaching, because it was a position of leadership. Other bans excluded women from holding money on deposit or serving as a legal guardian for either individuals or property. Neither could a family line be extended through women, passing instead only through men. Typically, Roman law treated the wife as the purchased property of her husband, leaving her virtually in the same situation as a slave. In both instances, the wife and slave were nothing more than chattel, existing solely for the man's benefit.

When it came to divorce, however, Roman law gave women virtual equality with their husbands. By the time Christianity became both legal and the official religion of the empire in the fourth century, women had the power to initiate divorce for virtually any reason. As time passed, divorce law relaxed to the point that "the wife had the absolute freedom to take the initiative and send her husband a divorce whenever and for whatever reason she wished."[8] Other rights and protections soon followed, but most of these came as a result of reforms introduced by Christian emperors.

Exception to the Rule: The Vestal Virgins

Roman law and tradition made one notable exception to legal and social restrictions on women: the Vestal Virgins (*sacerdos Vestalis*). The Vestal Virgins served as the holy priestesses of the goddess of fire or the hearth, Vesta, or Hestia in Greek mythology. Within the entire religious system, which included many gods, goddesses, and temples, the Vestal Virgins were the only women accorded the honor of performing duties of priestesses. These women played the key role of keeping the sacred fire of Vesta lit and supplied with fuel. This fire burned continually within the Temple of Vesta, located in the Roman Forum.

In Roman society, women were forbidden from taking part in the political process; they could not vote, hold office, or become citizens. The exception to this rule was the Vestal Virgins, who were the keepers of the sacred fire of Vesta, the Roman goddess of hearth, home, and family. These women could vote and own property. Here, Italian Baroque artist Ciro Ferri depicts the Vestal Virgins in this mid-seventeenth-century painting.

The Vestal Virgins reaped many benefits for performing their religious rites. Roman society honored them and bestowed on them rights and privileges usually reserved for men. Originally, there were two Vestal Virgins, but the number increased to four and then six in later periods. Chosen by lot, women served terms of 30 years. During the first 10 years they received instruction, the next 10 years they served, and the last 10 years they taught the newer Vestals.

During their service, the women carried out various religious rites and carefully maintained the fire. Many of these rites celebrated aspects of domesticity, such as the annual June 15 ceremonial sweeping out of the temple. Citizens of Rome could approach the temple and receive embers for their own home. Thus, the fire of Vesta literally served all of Rome. The continually burning fire also symbolized the health of Rome. If anything interrupted the maintenance of the fire, Romans believed the disruption foretold some impending calamity or misfortune. Allowing the fire to die out was a serious offense, punishable by death.

Perhaps the most interesting aspect of the Vestal Virgins was the way in which the legal code made exceptions for them. These priestesses enjoyed rights other Roman women did not, such as the ability to vote, own property, and write a will. Officially, their integrity led to the practice of entrusting to their care valuable public documents, such as treaties and wills. To inflict injury on one of these women, even accidentally, was an offense punishable by death. In all public venues, the Vestal Virgins enjoyed places of honor and special privilege. In short, the women who served as Vestal Virgins held a celebrity status unlike any other women of their time; they were, quite literally, exceptions to the laws.

WOMEN'S RIGHTS THROUGH THE MIDDLE AGES

With the rise of the rule of Christian emperors in Rome, the status of women improved. From the time of the emperors Constantine to Justinian (A.D. 313 to 565), changes were implemented that reflected the tenets of the Catholic Church. Most notably, modifications ended divorce on demand, as the state took steps to protect the marriage union. Some of these steps included requiring a priest for a valid marriage ceremony and placing restrictions on second and third marriages. Inheritance protections, custody rights, and safeguards to a woman's dowry also emerged in the legal code. Other changes reinstituted protections for women based on the idea that women were weaker than men. The legal situation for women under the Christian emperors changed, but not always for the better. For example, women faced higher levels of accountability before the law, but they still lacked true political equality with men.

In other ways, though, the legal code began to treat women more equitably. Over time, emphasis on equality diminished many of the legal inequities between men and women, especially in business and property rights. By the end of Justinian's reign, in the middle of the sixth century, women enjoyed many of the same legal protections and privileges that men enjoyed. Although these changes did not deliver full equality for women, legal reforms did provide some relief. Significantly, the legal protections that did exist guaranteed a large degree of independence for women in the latter periods of the empire. Despite these gains, women still lacked political equality. Thus, all rights and protections they enjoyed were subject to the authority of the male ruling class.

After the fall of Rome in A.D. 476, women continued to face legal discrimination. Many Roman practices that limited the private and public rights of women continued. Roman influence is evident in English legal code in use when jurist Sir William Blackstone published his *Commentaries on the Laws of England* (1765–1769), the compilation of English common law. Blackstone's work served as the basis for American law, and the later laws inherited many of the provisions for gender discrimination.

WOMEN'S RIGHTS IN ENGLAND BEFORE THE NINETEENTH CENTURY

The laws, traditions, and political institutions of England served as the primary model for the United States. Therefore, an examination of how England treated women in the legal code is appropriate to understand U.S. law. Women in England in turn enjoyed and were denied two kinds of rights: legal and political. Legal rights included matters considered private, such as property rights. Political rights included questions of public involvement, such as jury duty and suffrage. These distinctions provided the basic structure for early American legal tradition and statutes.

In general, throughout history, England treated single adult women "on practically a par with men so far as private rights are concerned."[9] These rights included such activities as owning property, entering into contracts, issuing a will, and filing lawsuits or being the subject of them. A woman could do each of these activities legally, without the interference or oversight of her father or some other male relative. Widows had rights of custody over their children. Inheritance rights, though, were another matter. Legal traditions often excluded women from inheriting property. Such a privilege was reserved primarily for men, except in rare circumstances. The English standard for inheritance did more than just favor men, however; it all but excluded women. Sir Blackstone addressed this legal question in the 1760s, when he wrote,

> In collateral inheritances the male stock shall be preferred to the female; that is, kindred derived from the blood of the male ancestors, however remote, shall be admitted before those from the blood of the female, however near; unless where the lands have, in fact, descended from a female. Thus, the relations on the father's side are

admitted *in infinitum* before those on the mother's side are admitted at all.[10]

Blackstone himself observes that English treatment of women, at least in matters of inheritance, was worse than women were treated in Roman times. Younger sons faced similar obstacles, as laws of primogeniture required that only the eldest received the property inheritance, thereby preserving family estates. On the other hand, as lopsided as the system was, it sometimes favored women. For instance, daughters or even granddaughters of the oldest son—in the event of the latter's death—received the property inheritance before the younger son (brother of the oldest son).

Once married, a woman soon learned that her husband held most of the rights. Common law essentially recognized the husband as "lord" of his family and thus obliged *"to correct and chastise his wife."*[11] This right to correct his wife included the power to confine her, a power not curtailed until the end of the nineteenth century. Aside from common law, the Catholic Church maintained authority over both marriage and divorce until the English Reformation in the 1530s. Ironically, divorce was one of the main issues that led King Henry VIII to dissolve English ties to the Catholic Church. After the Reformation, divorce became a state matter. Divorce literally required an act of Parliament. Thus, only the extremely wealthy and well connected attempted to obtain divorces. For most, legal separation was the best they could hope for, and then only in cases of desertion or adultery. In place of the Catholic Church, Parliament limited divorce rights through the Church of England.

As for public rights, English women had few. No woman could serve on a jury or in judgment for any legal proceeding. Voting was a privilege reserved for men (and until the nineteenth century, few men even enjoyed that right). Women were denied access to higher education. Thus, single women enjoyed some private rights (for example, property rights), but society denied all women most public rights until the nineteenth and twentieth centuries.

WOMEN'S RIGHTS IN THE AMERICAN COLONIES

When English settlers first came to the North American continent, they brought with them the social and legal traditions and institutions of their homeland. Many of these traditions "sought to negate the legal and social identity of women, leaving them to the care and supervision of their husbands and fathers."[12] The new continent offered the opportunity to form a new society. Instead, European settlers reestablished key elements of the old order in the new land. This new order asserted the political power of men within the system and institutions of government and excluded women from achieving power or influence.

The American Revolution offered the opportunity to alter the status quo for women. The revolutionary spirit certainly promised to deliver significant changes in American society. The Declaration of Independence emphatically proclaimed a belief in equality. The wording placed the limitation of "men" on its proclamation, failing to include women in the assertion of God-given equality. To the women's rights activists who came later, this unfortunate exclusion was a lost opportunity.

At the time, at least one woman recognized that independence from England presented the chance to right the inequalities embedded within society. In a letter dated March 31, 1776, Abigail Adams wrote a revolutionary statement to her husband, John, who was one of the leaders in the American Revolution. Sensing a break with England, she implored her husband to lead the way in framing a new kind

One of the first advocates for women's rights in colonial America was Abigail Adams, who is depicted here in an undated engraving from a painting by American artist Gilbert Stuart. Abigail implored her husband, John, to "Remember the Ladies" when he was helping to draft the Declaration of Independence.

of government and society. More than three months before the Declaration of Independence, Abigail's words, as radical as they were at the time, eloquently described a key issue that she thought the Continental Congress should consider. She wrote, "I desire you would Remember the Ladies, and be more generous and favourable to them than your ancestors. Do not put such unlimited power into the hands of the Husbands. Remember all Men would be tyrants if they could."[13]

Despite her pleas, her husband and the other delegates had no intention of reversing the norm for women. Many colonial American men disliked the way in which Parliament and King George III ruled over them. Few of those same men, however, had problems ruling over the women within the colonies.

John Adams answered his wife two weeks later, perhaps illustrating the prevailing male opinion at the time. Adams wrote, "As to your extraordinary Code of Laws, I cannot but laugh."[14] And, "Depend upon it, We know better than to repeal our Masculine systems."[15] When Adams and the other delegates signed the Declaration of Independence, the radical statement of equality specified men; American women would have to wait for their chance at equality.

Despite the apparent failure of the Continental Congress to improve the political status of women, representatives of the young nation also changed the language of its political foundations. In the decades following the American Revolution, political considerations for many social and political reform movements centered on the founding ideals of freedom, equality, and consent of the governed. The women's rights movement incorporated these ideals into their ideology to vindicate their cause. Indeed, the terminology of the American Revolution served the women's movement well. The Declaration of Independence itself served as the template for the women's rights leaders who met in Seneca Falls, New York, in 1848, to demand political equality.

WOMEN'S RIGHTS IN NINETEENTH-CENTURY AMERICA

In many respects, nineteenth-century American women had as few rights as those living in ancient Roman times. Power over women passed from fathers to husbands. Married women could not own property or enter into

WOMEN ON AMERICAN MONEY

Women have adorned American money since the founding of the new nation. Until 1979, though, all women depicted were allegorical representations of republican ideals, such as liberty. The Anthony dollar was minted in 1979–1981 and 1999. The U.S. government created the coin to honor Susan B. Anthony and her efforts to guarantee that American women had the right to vote. The U.S. Mint first released the Anthony dollar on July 2, 1979, in the city in which Anthony resided during her most politically active years: Rochester, New York.

The Anthony dollar, which was nearly the same size and color as the quarter, proved unpopular with the public. In the late 1990s, some vending machines (such as transit and postal machines) began accepting larger bills, then giving Susan B. Anthony dollars as part of the change, in anticipation of new $1 coins. Demand for the Anthony dollar grew, and the Treasury Department again minted the dollar coins for a single year in 1999.

Congress replaced the Anthony dollar in 1997, legislating the minting of a new gold-colored $1 coin. This new coin became the second American coin to depict the image of a real woman, first entering circulation in 2000. The coin bears a representative image of the Shoshone Indian guide to the Lewis and Clark Expedition, Sacagawea.

In December 2006, the U.S. Mint announced plans to pay tribute to the former first ladies by issuing commemorative $10 gold coins, beginning in 2007. The First coins, as they have been dubbed by the U.S. Mint, will be issued in conjunction with the Presidential $1 coins and will be minted four times each year. The front of the coins will include the following wording, familiar on all American coins: "In God We Trust" and "Liberty," as well as the years of the president's term(s). The obverse (back) will also feature the name and portrait of the first lady. The reverse side will also include distinctive designs celebrating some image representing the spouse's life and work, with the customary "E Pluribus Unum" and "The United States of America." Presidents who were unmarried while in office will display a depiction of Liberty consistent with those on coins during their term(s) in office.

business contracts without their husbands' blessing and signature. Women could not vote, nor could they expect to be educated as well as men. In short, American women were second-class citizens with few legal and no political rights.

Despite their lack of power, however, the emergence of two significant social movements paved the way for women to demand political equality. These movements were based on issues of morality, they relied upon women to operate them, and more important, they struck a chord with reform-minded Americans, increasing awareness of other social wrongs, including gender inequality. Thus, alcohol abuse and slavery served as a primary catalyst for early advocates of women's rights.

3

Temperance and Abolition

During the first half of the nineteenth century, reformers attacked the social evils of their day. These "evils" included a host of issues, ranging from educational opportunities to prison and hospital reform to temperance and abolition of slavery. The fights against alcohol and slavery were among the most important reform movements in the early years of the American republic. In the case of temperance, though, viewing alcohol as a blight on society was certainly not a novel idea. Instead, such a view was consistent with earlier periods in America's history.

ALCOHOL AS A SOCIAL EVIL

Since the earliest settlements, colonial Americans wrestled with the issues of alcohol consumption and alcohol abuse. Puritans viewed drunkenness as a sin and treated violators as outcasts. When family members failed to influence a drinker's behavior, Puritans adopted legal constraints to punish alcohol abuse. Moralists blamed drunkenness for crime, poverty, and poor health. Opponents of alcohol use and abuse used moral arguments to advance their cause, but throughout the nineteenth century, temperance supporters increasingly turned to government to deal with this problem. After all, it was women and children who usually paid the price for the alcohol addiction of a husband or father.

At the end of the colonial period, social restraints became less and less effective at curtailing alcohol abuse. The colonies were growing, and with growth, came change. As the colonial economy and population grew, it began to shift from a rural society to an urban one. The increased size and number of cities led to many social problems, including unemployment and crime, which in some cases could be attributed to alcohol use. The American Revolution did nothing to provide relief. Instead, it ushered in momentous changes to the government, the economy, and societal norms. Alcohol ceased to be a private issue as legal and social restraints were lifted, and troubling incidents involving alcohol escalated. The increase in problems led many reformers to offer solutions. One such reformer was perhaps the foremost and possibly the most recognized physician in America: Dr. Benjamin Rush.

One of the signers of the Declaration of Independence, Rush sought to counter the effects of alcohol. Rush believed that excessive consumption of alcohol damaged both the psychological and physical health of the drinker and that the resulting damage to society made alcohol abuse a public concern. His thoughts sparked a response when, in 1789, a group of about 200 Connecticut farmers established a temperance (moderation) association. Within a few years, other groups surfaced in several other states. The temperance issue proved relevant; temperance movements enjoyed more success and support than did the more rigorous view of prohibition (forbidding the consumption of alcohol). Unfortunately, temperance leaders misjudged public support, choosing to include other vices in their campaigns. The enlarged list of issues threatened to dilute the strength of the movement. In the first half of the 1820s, in fact, the temperance movement was in danger of dying out.

However, the momentum soon returned with the establishment of the American Temperance Society in 1826. A decade later, the movement boasted more than 1.5 million members, in local associations dedicated to stemming the evils of alcohol. The movement enjoyed widespread support, with some 8,000 organizations throughout the growing nation. Temperance activists did not realize it at the time, but their efforts would eventually lead to the widespread political involvement of women, changing American politics in dramatic ways. Supporters of temperance printed magazines, newspapers, and journals detailing the evils of alcohol. Protestant supporters worked through their churches to advocate their views.

As the new nation grew in size and population, American cities swelled with the influx of recent immigrants. By the 1830s, more and more immigrants came from countries other than England. These migrants often viewed and treated alcohol in ways counter to the dominant culture. The differences posed a threat to social order, which resulted in a growing interest in temperance.

In the 1830s, organized temperance groups continued to agitate within the political system. Their efforts lasted for a century and concluded with the 1919 ratification of a constitutional amendment prohibiting the sale, distribution, or possession of alcohol. But the movement's greatest contribution only had indirect ties to the issue of alcohol abuse. Temperance helped usher in a previously untapped resource in American politics: women.

FROM TEMPERANCE TO ABOLITION

Women served in leadership roles within the temperance movement. At the heart of temperance was the basic conviction that alcohol consumption and abuse was immoral. The collection of like-minded people who sought

One of the first crusades women rallied behind in the United States was that of the temperance movement. Here, women of the Temperance League are depicted destroying barrels of alcohol in this Currier & Ives lithograph titled *Woman's Holy War*.

to promote temperance inevitably led to the desire to strike down another evil institution: slavery. Slavery in nineteenth-century America was peculiar to the South, where intensive labor was required to raise and harvest agricultural crops such as tobacco and cotton.

William Lloyd Garrison, founder of *The Liberator*, a radical abolitionist newspaper, demanded immediate and uncompensated emancipation of all African-American slaves. This uncompromising approach served to split the abolitionist movement. Garrison was perhaps the most prominent and outspoken critic of American slavery in the 1830s. Garrison waged war with his pen against the evils of slavery. Most Americans were not abolitionists and were thus unprepared to follow such radical leadership. The moderate wing of the movement favored gradual emancipation and eventually found a home in the Republican Party, established in 1854. This faction opposed the extension of slavery, but fell short of calling for its complete abolition. The radical wing, led by firebrands such as Garrison, continued to insist on the end to slavery, sooner rather than later. The term *abolitionists* usually refers to this bloc after the late 1830s.

Much like the temperance movement, the abolitionist movement enjoyed fervent support from religious-minded individuals who wanted to cure a social evil. Many people within the abolitionist movement, both men and women, were generally reform-minded, and they supported causes such as improving prisons and asylums, funding education publicly, and, of course, temperance. One reform issue drove a wedge between many reformers, however—the issue of women's rights. On that issue, there was little agreement and nearly no way to compromise. The issue surfaced in the 1830s and eventually resulted in a split among abolitionists.

The abolitionist movement attracted many women to the cause, although many of these organizations banned women from becoming members. Consequently, women opposed to slavery promoted abolition, but they did so at first in a supporting role, then later in larger roles within their own societies. The role of women within the established, male-dominated groups led to friction among

"WHAT IS POSSIBLE FOR ME IS POSSIBLE FOR YOU"

Born a slave in 1818, Frederick Augustus Washington Bailey later escaped and became a world-renowned orator and champion of human rights. Raised in the slave state of Maryland, he became a skilled boat worker. His owner allowed him some freedoms, but Frederick desired true freedom. In 1838, at age 20, he escaped by borrowing some papers of a free black sailor and going first to Philadelphia, then New York City. Once there, he married a free black woman he had met in Baltimore before the couple relocated to New Bedford, Massachusetts. To protect his freedom, he changed his last name to Douglass.

In 1841 William Lloyd Garrison, the unwavering abolitionist, hired Douglass as a lecturer and writer for the Massachusetts Anti-Slavery Society. In this role, Douglass's natural gift for oratory became readily apparent. He amazed and entertained audiences with his personal stories and denunciation of slavery. He later toured England, where, in 1846, admirers raised the necessary funds to purchase his freedom from Hugh Auld, who still held legal rights of ownership over him.

Now free, Douglass and his family moved to Rochester, New York, where he began to publish his own abolitionist paper, *The North Star*. He continued to promote abolition. He also attended the Women's Rights Convention held in 1848 in Seneca Falls, New York, where he signed

members and leadership, as most men opposed women speaking publicly to mixed audiences (men and women). The abilities of several talented female leaders, however, led to their rise within abolitionist circles. Regardless of the tensions, perhaps the most important impact of abolitionism was "women's gradual movement from the private to the public sphere."[16] Opportunities for activism within the abolitionist movement eventually led to the

the Declaration of Sentiments. He supported women's rights and encouraged activists to fight for suffrage. Later, during the Civil War, he promoted emancipation as a goal worthy of waging war. He also actively recruited for the 54th Massachusetts Regiment, which was made up entirely of African-American volunteers, including two of Douglass's sons. Following the Civil War, Douglass moved to Washington, D.C., where he served in various honorary and governmental roles, including United States Marshal for the District of Columbia, Recorder of Deeds for Washington, D.C., and Minister-General to the Republic of Haiti.

Throughout his life, Douglass often said, "What is possible for me is possible for you."[*] Douglass personified the message he shared with so many throughout his life. To realize their dreams, Douglass encouraged others to "Believe in yourself," "take advantage of every opportunity," and "use the power of spoken and written language to effect positive change for yourself and society."[**] Frederick Douglass lived by these mottoes, and the changes he helped bring about in American society included rights for ex-slaves and eventually for women. Indeed, what was possible for him, became possible for women; specifically, gaining the right to vote.

[*] "A Short Biography of Frederick Douglass." Available online at http://www.frederickdouglass.org/douglass_bio.html
[**] Ibid.

acceptance of women as public speakers to groups of men and women. Ironically, the promotion of women's rights became the catalyst for division within the abolitionist movement.

Women's rights became a prominent issue because some of the most committed, influential, and persuasive leaders opposed to slavery were women. Many of these women were religious, and they were convinced of the righteousness of their cause. One such female leader within the abolitionist movement came from a most unlikely place: a Quaker family from Puritan New England. Her name was Lucretia Mott.

LUCRETIA COFFIN MOTT

Lucretia Coffin Mott was the most prominent female reformer of the early nineteenth century and first American feminist. She was the second of seven children, born January 3, 1793, in Nantucket, Massachusetts. Her prominent family belonged to the Religious Society of Friends, or Quakers. Family and Quaker tradition shaped the future activist. Mott later said, "I grew up so thoroughly imbued with women's rights that it was the most important question of my life from a very early day."[17] This focus on women's rights helped her realize the importance of unity within the women's rights movement when sharp disagreements arose. At 13, Lucretia left home to attend the Nine Partners Boarding School, a Quaker-run academy near Poughkeepsie, New York. This school offered a plan of study equivalent to a high-school education—the highest level of instruction women could receive at that time. Lucretia completed her coursework and, upon graduation, was qualified to teach. Later, she taught at Nine Partners, where the relevance of women's rights to her life was soon revealed. She learned that male teachers earned twice the amount as their female counterparts performing the same duties. She never forgot this inequity and strove to resolve similar disparities.

In 1811, Lucretia married another teacher at the school, James Mott. Lucretia then began visiting different Quaker meetinghouses, acting as a traveling speaker. Quakers treated women more like equals than did the rest of American society and allowed women to speak in public. In 1821, the couple moved to Philadelphia, where they were able to engage in more political activism. Both James and Lucretia shared the same loathing of slavery and actively participated in abolitionist activities. James Mott was a member of the American Anti-Slavery Society. Biases prohibited Lucretia from also joining the society, so she decided to start her own group, the Philadelphia Female Anti-Slavery Society. She utilized her gift for oratory, making speeches in support of abolition. In so doing, she became one of the first Quaker women to promote the cause of abolition. Quaker men had opposed slavery for some time, but women were not typically involved in the fight for abolition.

At one point, the Motts became involved in a rift within the Quakers. In the Great Separation of 1827, they chose to side with the more liberal segment, led by Elias Hicks. The Hicksite group favored a more open-minded and mystical approach to Quakerism, as opposed to the more traditional beliefs. Specifically, Hicks advocated the supremacy of one's own Inner Light over that of the Bible. This approach appealed to the Motts. The Hicksite branch also held slavery to be one of the greatest evils, another view shared by the Motts.

After choosing sides in the Great Separation, Lucretia spoke regularly in favor of abolition throughout the East and the Midwest, especially at Quaker meetings. She also spoke to groups such as the Anti-Slavery Convention of American Women and the Non-Resistance Society. She pleaded for abolition, but she also implored her audience to push for wider social and moral reforms. Mott effectively helped found two additional antislavery organizations in the 1830s, a testament to her desire to end slavery.

True to her Quaker roots, Mott also opposed slavery in practical, everyday ways. She and her husband refused to purchase, use, or consume any goods produced by slaves, including cane sugar and cotton cloth. Mott, believing

Lucretia Mott was one of the leading abolitionists and women's rights advocates of the first half of the nineteenth century. However, she did not gain notoriety until she published *Discourse on Woman*, a book that detailed the restrictions women faced in American society. Here, American photographer Frederick Gutekunst captures Mott in this 1862 photograph that is today on display at the National Portrait Gallery in Washington, D.C.

the government could be wrong, observed, "We too often bind ourselves by authorities rather than by the truth."[18] Mott and her husband chose to follow their beliefs, and disobeyed federal fugitive slave laws by providing refuge for runaway slaves in their home. They thus demonstrated a full commitment to abolition.

THE GRIMKÉ SISTERS

Other women also helped lead the fight against slavery. Two of the most colorful female abolitionists were the Grimké sisters of South Carolina. Sarah Grimké and her sister Angelina were born in Charleston, but both became Quakers and moved to Philadelphia in the late 1820s. The Grimké sisters were outspoken opponents of slavery; because their family owned many slaves, they personally witnessed its effects. After moving north, they traveled throughout the region in the 1830s, lecturing on the evils of slavery and the need for social reform. The two sisters were among the first women to speak to mixed audiences in public. Many looked down on the women for daring to speak to audiences that included men. The sisters often endured scathing insults and public mistreatment. Their experiences convinced them of the need to gain and protect women's rights.

Angelina married renowned abolitionist, Theodore Weld in 1838. The two intended for Angelina to continue promoting abolition, but the stress of maintaining a household and having three children limited her involvement. Her sister Sarah moved in with her, helping with the domestic chores of a growing family. The sisters practically retired from their public activism, but both continued to defend abolition and women's rights through their writing. Both women edited a collection of southern newspaper stories detailing slavery in *American Slavery as It Is: Testimony of a Thousand Witnesses*, published in 1839. These articles included descriptions of elderly slaves "inhumanly cast out in their sickness and old age, and must have perished but for the kindness of their friends."[19] Such narratives helped raise public awareness of the injustices produced by slavery. The Grimké sisters also advocated civil disobedience if a law violated a higher moral principle. In the words of Angelina, "If a law commands me to sin I will break it; if it calls me to suffer, I will let it take its course unresistingly."[20] The two women also contributed articles, letters, and other commentary supporting abolition and women's rights.

FROM ABOLITION TO WOMEN'S RIGHTS

Both Lucretia Mott and fellow women's rights advocate Elizabeth Cady Stanton attended the International Anti-Slavery Convention held in London, in June 1840. Because she was a woman, the convention did not recognize Mott as a delegate and refused to seat her. She joined Stanton and others behind a curtain at the gathering. Mott was allowed to address the convention, however. Significantly, Mott and Stanton met one another at the convention and discovered they shared similar dreams for women's rights. The two became friends and decided to organize a meeting to promote women's rights once they returned to the United States. It would be another eight years before they realized this goal. In 1848, they organized the first women's rights convention in Seneca Falls, New York. It was there that Lucretia and James Mott signed the Declaration of Sentiments. The Motts were instrumental in the Seneca Falls Convention—James served as chair of the convention and Lucretia gave the opening and closing lectures.

One significant issue in which Mott and Stanton disagreed, however, was that of divorce. Stanton favored the expansion of divorce rights for women, as a means of safeguarding women. Mott, however, opposed divorce and did not advocate any major changes to divorce codes, believing such action would result in more divorces. Despite their differing opinions on some matters, Mott and Stanton both believed that something needed to be done to improve women's rights.

Mott did not limit herself to the causes of abolition and women's rights. She also promoted world peace, serving in the Universal Peace Union, which was established in 1866. In 1867, Mott joined others who headed west to Kansas to campaign for female and black suffrage. Mott's activism was not limited to social and political arenas. She also joined a group of religious reformers, including American poet Ralph Waldo Emerson, who, in 1867, started the Free Religious Association, a group that supported a rationalist approach to theology and religion.

Despite all her work, Mott was not well known until after the 1850 publication of her *Discourse on Woman*. This book described the social and legal limitations women faced in the United States. Other ventures for this pioneering woman included helping establish Swarthmore College in 1864. In 1866, Mott, together with Elizabeth Cady Stanton, Susan B. Anthony, and Lucy Stone founded the American Equal Rights Association. Mott served as the association's first president. The issue of black suffrage, without the advancement of female suffrage, divided many in the movement, however. When a rift developed between Lucy Stone (who supported foregoing female suffrage for a time to support black suffrage) and Stanton and Anthony (both of whom insisted on both black and female suffrage), Mott personally intervened to end the infighting, calling for unity within the movement in order to achieve the higher goal. Having become one of the leaders of the women's rights movement, she continued to support the effort until her death in 1880. Throughout her later years, Mott often used letters to help calm tensions among the movement's leaders, preserving much of the internal harmony of the movement.

NECESSARY EXPERIENCE

The efforts of Lucretia Mott and other women who established their own abolitionist organizations had some unforeseen side effects. One historian, Miriam Sagan, identifies two important lessons women learned as they operated separate nonmale abolitionist societies: how to organize and speak publicly. First, women discovered "a great deal about political organizing" as they conducted the work of managing a political organization.[21] Such an undertaking required organizational skills, as well as the ability to enlist the aid of volunteer workers. Women's societies organized their own campaigns, held their own conventions, and performed all the other tasks vital in maintaining these organizations. Women led these societies and spoke at their gatherings to promote their cause. Women wrote and circulated petitions and women dealt with the press. The female leaders of these groups engaged the opposing side in public debates and served as the mouthpieces for their cause.

Perhaps the "most important skill that women developed within the abolitionist movement was the art of public speaking."[22] This is significant because women of that era had few opportunities to gain experience in public speaking. A woman disposed "to speak publicly was considered immodest and irreligious at best; at worst, she was said to have committed a crime against society and God."[23] The value of this experience cannot be overstated. Women learned how to speak well and deliver their political message in the same manner in which other political messages of the day were communicated. Well-organized grassroots campaigns and public speeches eventually helped win women the right to vote, and women first gained their prowess in this area while they were involved with the abolitionist movement.

The Grimké sisters and Lucretia Mott helped raise awareness that women could promote political activism. Their work forged the path for other women, younger than themselves. It was one of those younger women who caused the spark that ignited the women's rights movement. That woman was Elizabeth Cady Stanton.

The Life of a Leader

Elizabeth Cady Stanton

One of the most important figures in the nineteenth-century American women's rights movement was Elizabeth Cady Stanton. This social activist made contributions that were invaluable in the fight for political equality for women. She was a driving force behind the first women's rights convention, held in Seneca Falls, New York, in 1848. Historians point to the Declaration of Sentiments, primarily written by Stanton, and presented at that convention, as the inspiration for women's rights issues, especially suffrage.

"I WISH YOU WERE A BOY!"

The story of Elizabeth Cady Stanton illustrates the need for reform and the long fight necessary to achieve it. Elizabeth was born November 12, 1815, in Johnstown, New York. She was the eighth of 11 children born to Daniel Cady and Margaret Livingston Cady. Of the 11 children, only 6 survived into adulthood, and one of those (a brother) died at age 20. Elizabeth and the four remaining children were all girls.

Elizabeth's father was a leading attorney who also held public office, serving in the New York State Assembly and one term as a Federalist member of the U.S. House of

Thanks to her father, who was a prominent attorney and judge, Elizabeth Cady Stanton developed an interest in women's rights after she came to realize how much the law favored men. Stanton is depicted in this National Woman Suffrage Association illustration at the first women's rights convention held at the Wesleyan Methodist Chapel in Seneca Falls, New York, in July 1848.

Representatives (1815–1817). Cady enjoyed a distinguished career in law, working as a young attorney with several noteworthy individuals, including Alexander Hamilton and Aaron Burr. At the close of his career, he even worked on a case with Abraham Lincoln. In 1847, Daniel Cady won appointment to the New York Supreme Court, where he served until 1855.

Elizabeth's father had a profound influence on her life. It was in his study that the future suffragist first realized that the law treated men and women differently. When still a young girl, Elizabeth discovered that married women had virtually no property rights. At the time, laws usually passed those rights on to the husband or a son. She also learned that women lacked other rights enjoyed by men, such as custody rights and protections in employment. For Elizabeth, these wrongs had to be made right, and she dedicated her life to addressing these inequities.

Another key influence on Elizabeth stemmed from the loss of so many Cady children. This manifested itself in different ways. The death of Eleazar, Elizabeth's older brother, at age 20, as he prepared to graduate from Union College, greatly affected the Cady family dynamics. Daniel Cady became despondent over the death of his son. In the aftermath of Eleazar's death, 11-year-old Elizabeth tried to console her father. As she offered comfort, her father displayed a common attitude of the day when he said, "Oh my daughter, I wish you were a boy!"[24] Trying to please her father, the young girl answered, "I will try to be all my brother was."[25] Despite Elizabeth's desire to please her father, Daniel Cady became more and more depressed. The rejection devastated Elizabeth, and it appeared she might become a victim herself in the aftermath of her brother's death.

A neighbor, the Reverend Simon Hosack, reached out to the young girl. He encouraged her to develop her intellect.

Considering American society at the time, this was not only compassionate, but bold: Women simply did not receive much of an education, because many people believed that women did not need much of an education. For Elizabeth, the gesture was well-timed. Her father's lack of appreciation for her seemed to be beyond her control. After all, she could not change the fact that she was not a boy. In contrast, Hosack affirmed her and her aptitude for learning. The reverend encouraged her reading and taught her Greek. Upon his death, he left her his Greek lexicon and other books. Perhaps more than any other individual, Reverend Hosack's support and encouragement gave Elizabeth the validation she needed to believe in herself.

Elizabeth's mother, Margaret Livingston Cady, simply could not bear the heartache of losing her children. The grieving mother was emotionally uninvolved with Elizabeth. Despite her mother's emotional distance and lack of parental involvement, Elizabeth later described her mother as "queenly."[26] Elizabeth's father absorbed himself in his work, cutting off his daughters from a parental relationship with him. So, individuals other than her parents played important roles for Elizabeth during much of her upbringing.

Elizabeth's older sister by 11 years, Tryphena, and her husband, Edward Bayard, provided much needed guidance and support for the future women's rights advocate. Bayard came from an influential family; his father served in both the U.S. House of Representatives and the U.S. Senate. Bayard studied law as an apprentice under Daniel Cady in his law office. Bayard's presence in Elizabeth's life was important because he held progressive views about women's legal rights.

Another event had an important impact on Elizabeth: Her family owned a slave, Peter Teabout, who later worked as a freeman for the Cadys. Peter, who performed the duties of babysitter and nanny, was responsible for Elizabeth and her sister Margaret. When Peter took the girls with him to his church, the two girls sat with him in the back because blacks were not permitted to sit in the front with whites. This and similar experiences helped open Elizabeth's eyes to the evils of discrimination and slavery, from which the women's rights movement was spawned.

One last person to influence Elizabeth during her younger years was her cousin Gerrit Smith of Peterboro, New York. The Smith home was a gathering place for social

A VINDICATION OF THE RIGHTS OF WOMEN

Years before Elizabeth Cady Stanton embarked on her quest, Mary Wollstonecraft, an Anglo-Irish feminist, was one of the first female writers to publish her thoughts on women's rights. Her book, *A Vindication on the Rights of Women*, published in 1792, remains an influential feminist writing today. In it, Wollstonecraft promoted the idea of sexual equality in society, including economic, political, and religious equality. She argued that education was the key to gaining true equality. In her book, she also advocated educational opportunities for women, arguing that through education women could achieve self-realization. She also challenged the common view that women were weak and feeble beings in need of protection from society. Her thoughts inspired many of the leaders who later fought for women's rights in the United States, including Elizabeth Cady Stanton and Susan B. Anthony.

Wollstonecraft supported the notion of female equality for personal reasons: She had lived through circumstances that made a lasting impression upon her. She was born in 1759 in London, the second of six children who suffered at the hands of an abusive, alcoholic father. She left home at 19 and later helped her sister Eliza successfully elude an abusive husband while arranging for a legal separation. She and Eliza later founded a school in Newington Green.

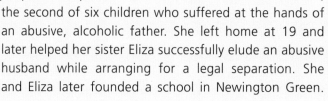

reformers. Elizabeth's visits there exposed her to many reformers and ideas. During one of her stays, she met her future husband.

AN EDUCATION IN A MAN'S WORLD

In the early nineteenth century, most women received little formal education. Elizabeth was one of the exceptions. She enrolled in Johnstown Academy, studying mathematics, Greek, and Latin. She also learned to play chess, despite

A true individualist, Wollstonecraft entered into a common-law marriage in 1794. The two had a daughter, but her husband left her in 1795. The experience further convinced Wollstonecraft of the need for legal protections for women. She believed that women would never realize such rights without adequate educational opportunities. In 1796, she renewed a friendship with fellow writer William Godwin. The relationship deepened, and the two became lovers. Both were opposed to marriage, however, believing it to be an institution of female oppression. An unplanned pregnancy changed their thinking. Discovering Mary was expecting a baby, the two decided to marry in March 1797. Sadly, just two weeks after giving birth to the child, a daughter, Wollstonecraft died of complications from a persistent infection. Godwin raised the child, named Mary, as well as Wollstonecraft's daughter. Mary grew up and married poet Percy Bysshe Shelley. In 1818, she published *Frankenstein*.

Although Wollstonecraft's own life was both tragic and brief, her writings raised issues virtually unaddressed before her time. Her work aroused feminist consciousness in other women in England, as well as in the United States. Many of her ideas concerning the spheres of political and domestic lives, private and public lives, and men and women still reverberate in modern political philosophy and thought. Her legacy is one that vindicates her belief in the equality of men and women.

the prevailing belief that the game was too complicated for girls. Elizabeth excelled at her studies, completing the requirements for graduation at age 16. Then, much to her dismay, she discovered that Union College, located in nearby Schenectady, New York, only admitted men. Determined to continue her studies, Elizabeth went to Troy, New York, enrolling in Troy Female Seminary (later renamed Emma Willard School, in honor of its founder, who taught there when Elizabeth attended it).

While Elizabeth was a student at Troy, the teachings of a revivalist preacher, Charles Grandison Finney, affected Elizabeth and her view of religion. As in her childhood, her concern for her spiritual well-being led her to worry about the fate of her soul. She later wrote, "Fear of judgment seized my soul. Visions of the lost haunted my dreams. Mental anguish prostrated my health."[27] Family members grew concerned and finally intervened, helping her find peace with herself. Her father, sister, and brother-in-law, Edward Bayard, accompanied her on a six-week trip to Niagara Falls. While traveling, the group read and discussed several works written by freethinking authors. For Elizabeth, these readings were "all so rational and opposed to the old theologies."[28] The dialogue with her family helped her sort things out, leaving her without fear of eternal damnation. From that time on, Elizabeth rejected organized religion, instead relying on logic and a humanitarian outlook to direct her conduct and thinking.

MARRIED REFORMER

Elizabeth Cady first met Henry Brewster Stanton while visiting her cousin Gerrit Smith in Peterboro, New York. Smith was an avid abolitionist, and later a member of the Secret Six—a group of wealthy northerners who funded

John Brown's raid on the federal arsenal at Harper's Ferry, Virginia in 1859. Stanton was a social activist, especially dedicated to the abolition of slavery. He served as an executive for the American Anti-Slavery Society. Stanton was a renowned orator and competent writer, talents he utilized in a professional career that included journalism, law, and politics. Prior to the Civil War, Stanton was regarded as the premier antislavery lecturer. When the two announced their engagement in 1839, however, Elizabeth's family opposed the marriage.

The Cadys were typically open-minded, but they had reservations about of the union because of Stanton's abolitionist ties. As one historian explains, "The Cadys supported religious benevolence and even temperance, but they regarded the abolitionists as fanatics."[29] Elizabeth buckled under the pressure. After arriving home in Johnstown, she broke the engagement. Stanton and Cady continued to correspond, however, and it was not long before Elizabeth changed her mind.

Despite her family's objections, Elizabeth Cady agreed to marry Henry Brewster Stanton in May 1840. With the exception of Elizabeth's sister Margaret, the Cady family did not attend the cermony. Elizabeth insisted that the wedding vows include no pledge to obey her husband. The minister complied, and the two were married. Many other nineteenth-century feminists followed her example when they married. The day after the ceremony, the couple went to New Jersey, where they visited renowned abolitionists Theodore Dwight Weld and his wife, Angelina Grimké Weld. After their visit there, the Stantons continued to New York City and left for an eight-month honeymoon in Europe, where Henry was to serve as a delegate to the June 1840 World Anti-Slavery Convention in London.

Despite the fact that their father was a slaveholder, Angelina Grimké Weld and her sister Sarah Moore Grimké became staunch abolitionists. In 1835, Angelina (above) wrote an anti-slavery letter to fellow abolitionist William Lloyd Garrison, who published it in his newspaper *The Liberator*. Titled "An Appeal to the Christian Women of the South," the letter made Angelina a pariah in the South, and she was threatened with arrest if she ever returned to her native South Carolina.

SEXISM WITHIN ABOLITIONISM

When Elizabeth Cady Stanton and other women tried to take part in the 1840 World Anti-Slavery Convention held in London, sexism prevailed. A sharp disagreement broke out concerning whether or not women could be admitted as members of the convention. Intense debate ensued, which resulted in female delegates, elected by the organizations they represented, not being allowed to participate in the proceedings. The vote forced women to sit silently behind a curtain, as unseen observers and listeners, but not as contributing members of the convention. William Lloyd Garrison, arriving after the decision was reached, showed his solidarity with the women by refusing his seat, choosing instead to sit with the women in roped off and obscured seats.

Something positive came from the experience, however: Elizabeth Cady Stanton and Lucretia Mott met and developed a friendship. The two spent time together in London, seeing the sights and discussing the lack of women's rights. Before leaving London, Stanton and Mott agreed to work together on women's rights issues in the United States. At the conclusion of the antislavery convention, Elizabeth and Henry completed their honeymoon. Then, the newlyweds adjusted to their new life together.

MARRIED LIFE

Upon their return from Europe, the couple lived with Elizabeth's parents while Henry, who by this time had become accepted by Elizabeth's family, studied law as an apprentice to his father-in-law. While in Johnstown, Elizabeth gave birth to the first of their seven children. Then, in 1843, Henry moved his wife and child to Boston, where he became a member of a law firm. The continuous flow of people in and out of Boston for abolitionist meetings delighted Elizabeth. It was in Boston where she had the opportunity to meet and form friendships with some of America's most prominent social activists of the day, including William Lloyd Garrison,

Frederick Douglass, Ralph Waldo Emerson, Robert Lowell, and Louisa May Alcott.

When Elizabeth married Henry Stanton, she did not follow the custom of the day and replace her surname with that of her husband's. Instead, she added it to her name, going by Elizabeth Cady Stanton. She also objected to being called Mrs. Henry B. Stanton. She believed that each woman had her own individual identity and keeping her surname intact preserved some of that identity. Other feminists adopted the practice.

Elizabeth's marriage was hardly trouble-free. Both Elizabeth and Henry traveled a great deal, meaning they spent more time apart than they did together. Although the two had similar personal dispositions, as well as aspirations for reform, they disagreed on the priorities of the reforms. Henry enthusiastically fought for the abolition of slavery, whereas Elizabeth increasingly poured herself into causes promoting women's rights. Despite their differences, the marriage endured, lasting 47 years until Henry's death in 1887.

FINDING A VOICE IN REFORM

Elizabeth Cady Stanton followed a course of action similar to most nineteenth-century female reformers: She joined other movements of the day, specifically the fights for abolition and temperance. Through these associations, Stanton learned valuable lessons about how to conduct a successful reform movement. She also met other prominent and talented individuals who shared her zeal for women's rights. The experiences also taught her valuable lessons about radicalism and public opinion. The friendships she forged and the knowledge she acquired proved invaluable to her ultimate goals of gaining rights for women.

Perhaps the most distinguishing characteristic of Elizabeth Cady Stanton's approach was her broad emphasis on women's rights. She emphatically believed in suffrage, but the right to vote was not the only issue on which she concentrated. Instead, she expanded her stance and struggled to change laws that affected women, especially married women. These laws addressed such issues as employment rights, divorce rights, property rights of women, restrictions of women's custody rights, and a controversial topic even then, abortion.

PERSONAL HARDSHIPS

Despite her reform-mindedness, Stanton faced many difficulties in her daily life. As mentioned, she became a mother, eventually having seven children, the last of whom was born in 1859. The pressures of maintaining a home, as well as bearing and raising children proved overwhelming at times. She preferred not to travel but still desired to remain active in the women's rights movement. Her obligations as a wife and mother made her involvement difficult. Although her children accompanied her on the rare occasions she traveled in support of women's rights, others—even within the movement—often accused her of not caring for her children when she gave lectures.

Her husband's mental health also affected Elizabeth and her advocacy. Hoping to find relief for Henry, in 1847, the Stanton family moved to Seneca Falls, New York. Elizabeth's father bought them a house in town. The move proved to be a difficult adjustment for Elizabeth. At 31 years old, the social activist found herself relegated to the domestic life of rural New York. Lacking the intellectual, social, and political stimulation she enjoyed in Boston, Elizabeth struggled to cope as she performed her household duties as wife and

In 1847, Elizabeth Cady Stanton and her husband, Henry Brewster Stanton, left Boston, Massachusetts, and moved to rural Seneca Falls, New York. Stanton's father, Daniel, bought them this house, where Elizabeth would discover the inequality that existed between men and women, as she had little time for anything else but raising her three children. Today, the house is part of the Women's Rights National Historical Park and is open to the public.

mother. To offset her boredom, the ever-restless Stanton did what she could, increasingly involving herself in local community affairs. Soon, she had built relationships with area women who held views similar to her own. Away from the hustle and bustle of Boston, Elizabeth Cady Stanton was about to help facilitate a national movement to reform the rights of women. And she did it from an improbable place: the rural community of Seneca Falls, in western New York.

5

Revolution

It was July 1848, and in the United States, "revolution was in the air."[30] Americans continued their tradition of reciting the Declaration of Independence in public squares, at picnics, and on courthouse lawns to commemorate the momentous break with Great Britain 72 years earlier. In 1848, revolution was more than an idea; it was spreading across Europe. Revolutionary spirit began in Sicily, and then swept north, from France to the German states. The 1848 revolution in France resulted in the end of their monarchy and the establishment of a republic, their second attempt at that form of government. Americans felt a kindred spirit with the French, especially during the month of July, when the U.S. citizens celebrated their own republic's birth with public ceremonies, parades, picnics, and fireworks. Yes, the spirit of revolution was alive and well in America in 1848.

That same spirit was also present in western New York, especially in Seneca Falls. The revolutionary attitudes in Seneca Falls manifested themselves in ways never before seen in the United States, however. This time, women led the way in articulating the purposes and aims of this revolutionary spirit.

THE IDEA IS BORN

On a warm July day in 1848, Elizabeth Cady Stanton arrived for tea at the home of a fellow reformer, Jane Hunt. She and her husband, Richard, who lived in Seneca Falls, were local Quakers hosting some special guests, including Lucretia Mott. Stanton's experiences and the hard work of her daily life convinced her that women needed to stand up for themselves. She later wrote "I poured out . . . the torrent of my long-accumulating discontent, with such vehemence and indignation that I stirred myself as well as the rest of the party to do and dare anything."[31] Indeed, the others shared in her resentment. For Stanton, the time for action was long overdue. She wrestled with societal expectations placed upon her as a woman. She was not sure what needed to be done, only that some action must be taken. Stanton later wrote of this personal realization and determination to organize a meeting for women's rights:

> The general discontent I felt with woman's portion as wife, housekeeper, physician, and spiritual guide, the chaotic conditions into which everything fell without her constant supervision, and the wearied, anxious look of the majority of women, impressed me with a strong feeling that some active measures should be taken to remedy the wrongs of society in general, and of women in particular. My experience at the World Anti-Slavery Convention, all I had read of the legal status of women, and the oppression I saw everywhere, together swept across my soul, intensified now by many personal experiences. It seemed as if all the elements had conspired to impel me to some onward step. I could not see what to do or where to begin—my only thought was a public meeting for protest and discussion.[32]

The group determined they would do something about their discontent. They decided to call a public meeting in order to protest the plight of women and discuss possible solutions. Before Stanton left the Hunt home that day, the date, time, and location for this women's meeting had been decided.

The group placed an unsigned advertisement in the *Seneca County Courier* on July 11. It read, "Woman's Rights Convention. A Convention to discuss the social, civil and religious condition and rights of Woman will be held in the Wesleyan Chapel, at Seneca Falls, N.Y. on Wednesday and Thursday, the 19th and 20th of July current, commencing at 10 o'clock a.m."[33]

The invitation was advertised to the public, but now a more formidable task lay before the women: how to organize and run a convention with barely a week to prepare.

The women eagerly set themselves to the task facing them. They decided to draw up a proclamation to present to the convention. They called this proclamation the Declaration of Sentiments. The document spelled out women's rights in much the same way the Declaration of Independence had specified the unalienable rights of American men to break away from the despotism of Great Britain. Each of the women played a part in the document, but it was Stanton who insisted that they pattern the statement after Jefferson's. This was deliberate, as Stanton hoped the familiarity of the Declaration of Independence would make it difficult to ignore the circumstances of women. Over the next several days, Stanton, with input from the others, worked on the Declaration of Sentiments.

Finally, the day arrived. A crowd of women stood outside the Wesleyan Chapel, but in their excitement they had forgotten to get the key. Stanton's nephew climbed through an open window and let the group into the building. The meeting started a little late, but when the convention opened, some 300 people had shown up, 240 of whom were women. Considering the short notice, the number of attendees was impressive. Although it lasted only two days,

Held at the Wesleyan Chapel in Seneca Falls, New York, on July 19–20, 1848, the Seneca Falls Convention was the first women's rights convention in the United States. Pictured here is the shell of the Wesleyan Chapel, which today is part of the Women's Rights National Historical Park.

the convention stirred a generation of women to promote change in American society.

SENECA FALLS

The first day's sessions of the two-day convention were supposed to be for women only but because so many men showed up, they were allowed to participate. However, when the proceedings began, the women faced a dilemma: Who should chair the convention? Women in that day did not presume to have such authority or stature. Even the female abolitionist societies at that time relied on men to act as their officers. Although the female organizers were self-confident, none of them had ever served in such a capacity. Lacking the necessary experience, the women pressed one of their husbands into service for the cause. James Mott, Lucretia's husband, agreed to preside over the proceedings as the chair of the convention. Thus, on the first day of the convention, only women were permitted to participate, but a male chair governed the proceedings.

On the first day, the time came for the presentation of the Declaration of Sentiments. Elizabeth Cady Stanton read the document to the attendees. She began, "We hold these truths to be self-evident; that all men and women are created equal." The addition of women in the midst of a familiar and cherished phrase radically altered its meaning. Instead of rebelling against a monarch, this new document made the case for a new revolution. In the words of one historian, this was to be a revolution "of women against patriarchal institutions: the law, the family, religion, work, education, and most startling of all, of politics."[34]

The Declaration of Sentiments included some of the same concepts brought forth by the Declaration of Independence, but the differences in the two dramatically stated the case for women's rights:

> But when a long train of abuses and usurpations, pursuing invariably the same object, evinces a design to reduce them under absolute despotism, it is their duty to throw off such government and to provide new guards for their future security. Such has been the patient sufferance of the women under this government, and such is now the necessity which constrains them to demand the equal station to which they are entitled.

Stanton and the other signers claimed equality with men. This revolutionary thought was followed by evidences that men had established "an absolute tyranny" over women, by listing those "injuries and usurpations" in the Declaration of Independence. These included the following:

1. Women had never been allowed to vote.

2. Laws for women were made by men.

3. Uneducated and corrupt men enjoyed the rights denied to women.

4. Lacking suffrage, women were oppressed by various laws.

5. Married women lacked rights to own property or keep her own wages.

6. Women were "compelled to promise obedience to her husband."

7. Divorce laws favored men over women.

8. Single women could own property but were forced to pay taxes, despite their lack of political rights.

9. Women faced wage inequity; certain professions were denied to women.

10. Women could not obtain a college education.

11. Men viewed women as subordinate in church and banned them from performing any public function of the church.

12. A higher standard of morality existed for women.

13. Men claimed powers over women that belonged to God.

14. Men have tried to convince women to remain dependent on men and a male-dominated society.

These grievances were every bit as radical as those written by Jefferson 72 years earlier. Stanton and the others made a bold statement with their declaration, a statement that indicated drastic changes needed to be made within the government and society.

In addition to the Declaration of Sentiments, Stanton also proposed a series of resolutions to the convention to consider for adoption. These resolutions addressed each of the grievances listed in their document. One of the resolutions, demanding that women be allowed to vote, was so radical that Stanton and her own husband argued about it. Although Henry Stanton agreed with the concept that women faced inequality without voting rights, he also believed incorporating the demand for suffrage in the resolutions was too revolutionary to benefit the movement. He felt that its inclusion would only lead to popular rejection of the women's rights movement. The two disagreed over the issue, with Henry threatening to leave the conference. Elizabeth stood her ground, convinced that suffrage was a fundamental right women must claim in order to gain equality. Elizabeth retained the suffrage measure in the Declaration of Sentiments, and Henry left the conference.

The suffrage resolution threatened to divide the convention, as many women were unsure whether it was a wise inclusion. Stanton appealed to the delegates to re-think the vote, "The right is ours. Have it we must. Use it we will. The pens, the tongues, the fortunes, the indomitable wills of many women are already pledged to secure this right."[35] Despite her pleas, the resolution appeared to lack the necessary support. Then, Frederick Douglass asked to speak. He implored the women to consider the power of voting, discussing how that power offered guarantees to their freedom and equality—the very rights they were demanding. His arguments helped persuade the attendees, and the suffrage resolution, like the others, passed.

At the conclusion of the convention, 100 individuals signed the Declaration of Sentiments—68 women and 32 men. Exclaiming "firmly relying upon the final triumph of the Right and True, we do this day affix our signatures,"

One of the attendees of the Seneca Falls Convention was social activist Frederick Douglass, who is depicted in this 1855 engraving by American artist John Chester Buttre. Douglass was instrumental in persuading the delegates to support suffrage, because he believed it would guarantee their freedom and equality.

signers thereby gave their approval to the declaration. Four decades later, Frederick Douglass contemplated their work at the convention, writing, "We were few in numbers, moderate in resources, and very little known in the world."[36] Douglass also commented, "The most we had to commend us, was a firm conviction that we were in the right, and a firm faith that the right must ultimately prevail."[37] The document, and the movement it supported, was indeed revolutionary. It was July 1848, and revolution was certainly in the air.

Reaction to the Declaration of Sentiments was both immediate and scathing. Editorials condemned the meeting and the declaration as subversive and impractical. The attacks were so derisive that some of the women asked to have their signatures removed. Stanton optimistically viewed the bad press as a blessing. She told Lucretia Mott, "It will start women thinking, and men, too, and when men and women think about a new question, the first step is taken."[38] For Stanton, the process of winning women's rights was about taking steps to reach the main objective. She understood that such a process took time.

The convention at Seneca Falls catapulted Stanton into the limelight. She attended and spoke at another women's rights convention, held the following month in Rochester, New York. The exposure cemented Stanton's place as a leader in the women's rights movement. She continued to meet more women who supported reform. She began traveling a little more, although she usually took her children with her. The seeds of a movement, having been planted, now needed to be watered. The much-needed water came in the form of a woman who ended up spending most of her life fighting for women's rights. Her name was Susan B. Anthony.

SUSAN B. ANTHONY

Susan Brownell Anthony was born February 15, 1820, in Adams, Massachusetts, to a father who was a farmer (later cotton textile mill owner) and abolitionist. She was the second of eight children born to Daniel, a practicing Quaker, and Lucy Read Anthony. Like Lucretia Mott, Susan's father followed the freethinking Elias Hicks in the Great Separation of 1827. Daniel was "so devout that toys, games, and music were all barred from his house for fear they might distract the children from what was called the Inner Light—the God who lived within every soul—and so committed to pacifism that he refused to vote or pay taxes to a government willing to wage war."[39] Equally important, Daniel believed in the Quaker conviction "that men and women were equal before God."[40]

Despite his devotion, Daniel also proved to be a nonconformist. When he married a non-Quaker—who never converted—he was forced to make a public apology

BLOOMERS

Nineteenth-century women's rights activist Amelia Bloomer was a friend of both Elizabeth Cady Stanton and Susan B. Anthony. In fact, she introduced the two in 1851. Bloomer began publishing her own newspaper, *The Lily*, in 1849. *The Lily* explored women's issues, especially those of temperance, education, suffrage, and fashion. It was in the area of fashion that Amelia left her most famous mark.

Women typically wore layers of clothing, much of it designed to accentuate their figures, while covering as much skin as possible. The customary female attire of the day included corsets, petticoats, and large hoop skirts. Corsets made with whalebones created an hourglass shape by compressing the waist. The hoops and petticoats added more weight to the garb, while the dresses themselves included long skirts composed of up to five yards of fabric. For many women, the clothing society expected them to wear was overly restrictive. All of this apparel made breathing a challenge, and "women often fainted" from wearing the corsets.*

Bloomer began to address questions of women's fashion in *The Lily* in 1851, in a series of articles advocating that women wear less restrictive clothes, specifically, knee-length dresses with ankle-length pants underneath them, paired with a loose-fitting blouse. Feminists quickly adopted the new look. Because of Amelia's strong support for the style, many called the combination *bloomers*. The moniker stuck, forever linking Amelia Bloomer with the fashion of nineteenth-to the Meeting (the local Quaker congregation). When he purchased and wore an attractive coat, the Meeting made him explain himself. Although looked down upon for these actions, Daniel maintained his membership in the Meeting until he opened a dancing school in his attic, as an alternative to secular dance halls, which were all located in taverns. He had even refused to allow his own children to dance, but the Meeting expelled him over the incident. As a result, the Anthony family moved to Battenville, New York, in 1826.

century feminism. American society did not embrace the new style, however. Instead, Bloomer and other women who adopted the attire faced ridicule and scorn. Many people believed bloomers were inappropriate and too outlandish for dignified women to wear. Soon, the mistreatment became too much for the women, even for feminist leaders such as Elizabeth Cady Stanton, who feared the attention diverted focus from the greater issues facing women. By the end of 1853, Stanton gave up wearing the outfit in public. Many other women's rights activists had already rejected bloomers and returned to wearing traditional clothing. Bloomer herself tired of the controversy and stopped wearing bloomers in public by the end of the 1850s. Thus, this early attempt to redefine women's fashion failed in the face of public opposition.

As for Amelia Bloomer, she continued to publish *The Lily* until 1854, when she sold the magazine in order to move with her husband to Council Bluffs, Iowa. Bloomer believed in the cause, but she also valued her family. She explained her decision, writing, "But the *Lily*, being as we conceive of secondary importance, must not stand in the way of what we believe our interest. Home and husband being dearer to us than all beside, we cannot hesitate to sacrifice all for them."**

* Miriam Sagan, *Women's Suffrage* (San Diego: Lucent Books, 1995), 39.

** D. C. Bloomer, *Life and Writings of Amelia Bloomer* (New York: Schocken Books, 1975), 189.

Susan's mother, Lucy, was a complex woman. In family life, she supported her husband and his religious views, even allowing her children to become Quakers, although she herself never converted. She explained that she did not become a Quaker because she was "not good enough."[41] Politically, Lucy was a progressive woman. In 1848, she attended the convention held in Rochester, New York (two weeks after the Seneca Falls Convention), where she was one of the many attendees to sign the Declaration of Sentiments. Like her husband, Lucy believed in acting on one's personal convictions and in promoting the value of each individual, regardless of gender.

Gifted, young Susan learned to read by age four. In her desire to read, however, she strained her eyes to the point they became crossed. Her right eye never really recovered, and she was self-conscious of its misalignment throughout the rest of her life. After moving to Battenville, Susan began attending the local public school. She did well in her studies until the male teacher refused to teach her, or any girl, long division. Her father came to the rescue, and pulled her out of the school. He then opened a home school for her and the young women working in his cotton mills. For a time, her father taught the classes himself. Later, he hired a string of different teachers. One of these, Mary Perkins, was well educated and "an independent, unmarried woman."[42] At 15, Susan had progressed in her studies to the point that she was teaching in home schools and later in the local public school, where men earned three to four times the pay of women performing the same job.[43]

In the fall of 1837, Daniel Anthony decided to send Susan to the same Philadelphia boarding school her older sister Guelma attended, Deborah Moulson's Female Seminary. Daniel "believed his daughters' usefulness—as well as their sense of self-reliance—would be enhanced by further education."[44] Deborah Moulson ran her school with strict rules and a harsh tenor, but she also offered one of the most comprehensive programs of study for girls in that day. Susan enjoyed her studies but grew homesick for her family. The financial Panic of 1837 ended her time at Moulson's, because the Anthonys could no longer afford to pay tuition. Her father went bankrupt, moved to another community (now called Center Falls, New York), and tried to start over.

Her father's financial woes forced Susan to take up teaching again, this time to survive financially and help pay her father's debts. She started at Eunice Kenyon's Friends' Seminary in New Rochelle, before leaving in 1846 to teach and assume the duties as headmistress of the female department at Canajoharie Academy, in Canajoharie, New York. Again, she faced sexual discrimination, earning about one-fourth the salary of men in similar positions, as was customary. She taught there until 1849, when she resigned in order to live with her parents, now in Rochester, New York.

The move to Rochester helped Susan B. Anthony establish herself as her own woman. She had already discarded the clothing of Quakers while teaching in Canajoharie. Now she left the Friends altogether, joining the Unitarian Church. Over the years, she continued to distance herself from organized religion, a gradual shift that resulted in criticism and charges of atheism. While in Rochester, she also participated in the local temperance movement, and she served as secretary for the Daughters of Temperance. This position provided her the opportunity to speak publicly in opposition to alcohol abuse. Like Stanton and other suffrage leaders, experiences in other reform movements provided opportunities to hone skills they would need later.

6

Temperance, Abolition, and Suffrage

The year 1851 marked the meeting of two female reformers, Elizabeth Cady Stanton and Susan B. Anthony. The two women supported temperance and abolition. Their introduction occurred almost by accident: A mutual acquaintance, Amelia Bloomer, introduced the two on a street corner in downtown Seneca Falls. Stanton and Anthony formed a friendship that lasted for the next 51 years, and it was a friendship that also galvanized the women's movement.

A KEY FRIENDSHIP

Anthony and Stanton first combined their collective energies to support temperance, although their names will be forever linked to their shared work for female suffrage. Although other women rose up to help lead the fight for suffrage, it was Anthony and Stanton who initiated the suffrage-related dialogue and other efforts in the latter half of the nineteenth century. The two played crucial roles in founding the Woman's State Temperance Society in 1852 in New York, although the organization folded the next year. Despite its brief existence, the society provided the platform for Stanton to address one of the overarching issues she supported: women's legal rights to and in divorce.

While president of the Woman's State Temperance Society, Stanton provoked outrage, even among the society's members, for claiming that drunkenness was grounds for divorce. American society, even those people—including women—who advocated for more women's rights, was not ready for such radical talk. Stanton persisted, although she did curtail public discussion of some of her extreme views, and with Anthony she increasingly shifted focus on the more fashionable and socially acceptable issue of a women's right to vote. Whereas both Anthony and Stanton believed in and fought for women's suffrage, temperance, and abolition, the elder Stanton also advanced wider-ranging and more radical goals for societal reform. Despite their minor differences, the two worked well together, and their alliance proved to be a virtually indestructible force within the women's rights movement.

When Anthony attended the 1852 women's rights convention in Syracuse, New York, her abilities as a public speaker propelled her into the limelight. She was justifiably seen as a capable advocate for women's rights. Rising to the challenge, Anthony soon dedicated herself to the cause of women's rights, and suffrage in particular.

To aid the cause, Anthony believed, as did many others at the time, that strong ties between abolition and suffrage only served to strengthen both movements. The plight of women and slaves was similar. Neither group held the rights of citizenship enjoyed by white men. In 1856, Anthony began working as the agent for the American Anti-Slavery Society for the state of New York. William Lloyd Garrison founded this organization, which was dedicated to the complete abolition of slavery. Anthony addressed the

Ninth National Woman's Rights Convention in New York City on May 12, 1859. In her speech, she linked the two movements when she posed the question, "Where, under our Declaration of Independence, does the Saxon man get his power to deprive all women and Negroes of their inalienable rights?"[45] To Anthony, slaves and abolitionists were natural allies to those involved in the fight for female suffrage.

A FORMIDABLE ALLIANCE

Elizabeth Cady Stanton and Susan B. Anthony made an impressive team, each making up for the other's weaknesses. Stanton was married and cared for her young children. Anthony was single, with no family obligations. Stanton, an accomplished orator, was gifted at constructing a fine speech. The problem was Stanton had neither the time nor the inclination to travel and speak. The younger Anthony had both the wherewithal and desire to travel and speak at rallies, conventions, and other kinds of meetings. Stanton lacked some of the interpersonal skills needed to manage a large movement. She also desired to see the movement encompass more than just suffrage. Anthony, however, knew how to coordinate the various factions and keep them focused on her preferred issue: women's suffrage. The two worked well together, despite some differences in opinion on which issues should take precedence within the movement. Ultimately, the friendship and working relationship proved to be effective and long lasting. Anthony seemed to understand her role in the relationship. On Stanton's death, the younger woman described their relationship this way: "When she forged the firebolts I fired them."[46] Anthony also wrote of Stanton, "I always called her the philosopher and statesman of our movement" and "a most finished writer" of the early women's rights movement.[47]

During the early 1850s, Susan B. Anthony began to campaign for women's suffrage with Elizabeth Cady Stanton. In 1869, the two women cofounded the National Woman Suffrage Association, which not only advocated a woman's right to vote but also worked to admit women into labor unions.

DIFFICULTIES FOR REFORMERS: THE BREAK FROM ABOLITION

The Civil War and the climax of abolitionism led to a rift within the women's rights movement. The debate pitted family member against family member. Both Susan B. Anthony and Elizabeth Cady Stanton (who broke ranks with her own husband, a leading orator for the cause of abolition), sought the defeat of the Fourteenth and Fifteenth amendments. These amendments granted citizenship to all black males (Fourteenth), and guaranteed these same men the right to vote (Fifteenth). Their opposition seems somewhat out of character, especially considering their opposition to slavery. To these women, however, the introduction of an entirely new group of men into the political process created a new set of problems for women's suffrage. Specifically, men already believed women should not be able to vote. Allowing more men to vote only raised the hurdle even higher as they fought to educate men on the inequities of denying suffrage to women. Stanton and Anthony did not actually oppose black suffrage. What they opposed was granting suffrage to black men but ignoring the voting rights of women—white and black women.

Understandably, Stanton was frustrated with abolitionist leaders, especially those in Congress. She and other suffragists had worked within abolitionists, fighting for the rights of slaves and women. Nevertheless, many within the Republican leadership believed that including women in the language of the Fourteenth and Fifteenth amendments would only serve to cloud the issue and doom the chances of gaining citizenship and suffrage for the freedmen. Stanton begged, threatened, and expressed disgust, all to no avail. The abolitionists refused to stipulate the inclusion of women in the amendments.

Congress passed the amendments on to the states, and Stanton withdrew her support for ratification, stating, "I will cut off this right arm of mine before I will ever work for or demand the ballot for the Negro and not the woman."[48] Later, Stanton recorded in her memoirs that she believed the partnership women had forged with abolitionists should have prevailed. After all, women and freedmen had endured many of the same political abuses in the past. "Women have stood with the Negro, thus far," she wrote, "on equal ground as ostracized classes, outside the political paradise; and now, when the door is open, it is but fair that we both should enter and enjoy all the fruits of citizenship."[49]

Elizabeth Cady Stanton did not want to see the two movements go their separate ways. She tried desperately to maintain the alliance between the abolitionists and those individuals who favored women's rights. Stanton's tolerance for inaction waned, however. In time, her language reflected racist attitudes: She argued that, as voting citizens, freed blacks and immigrants would bring their "pauperism, ignorance, and degradation" to the American political system.[50] To counteract these negative effects, she said, the franchise needed to be extended to female voters of "wealth, education, and refinement."[51] On another occasion, Stanton proclaimed that the amendments raised "a serious question whether we had better stand aside and see 'Sambo' walk into the kingdom [of civil rights] first."[52]

The success of black suffrage obviously distressed Stanton and others who had fought so hard for both abolition and female suffrage. Unfortunately, the arguments Stanton put forward may have contributed to division within the civil rights movement of the 1860s and 1870s.[53] The introduction of literacy tests for blacks to exercise voting rights did in fact soon follow this division, and later became a dominant feature of Jim Crow laws in the South.

Stanton was not alone in supporting universal suffrage. A leading member of the Radical Republicans, Thaddeus Stevens held the same view. The Pennsylvania congressman was a well-known firebrand for abolition and favored harsh requirements on the South during Reconstruction. Stevens also called for universal voting rights. In 1866, he introduced a petition to the House of Representatives calling for universal suffrage—this petition was drawn up by a group of suffragists, including Stanton and Anthony. Regardless of their endeavors, women were left out of the language of the Fourteenth Amendment, which Congress passed on to the states for ratification in June 1866. Just two years later, the three-fourths majority threshold was met: On July 9, 1868, Louisiana and South Carolina became the twenty-seventh and twenty-eighth states to ratify the amendment. The Fourteenth Amendment, which granted the rights of citizenship to black men, was now part of the Constitution.

Stanton's position on the issue of black suffrage had other effects, as well. Frederick Douglass and other civil rights leaders openly broke with Stanton because of her views. Douglass was empathetic, but believed Stanton did not see the bigger picture. To Douglass, women at least had indirect representation through family ties to their fathers and husbands. Under the Fourteenth and Fifteenth amendments, blacks could now have what women already enjoyed, albeit in a roundabout way.[54]

Despite having lost the fight to influence the Fourteenth Amendment, Stanton continued to argue against the Fifteenth Amendment, which states the right "to vote shall not be denied or abridged by the United States or by any State on account of race, color, or previous condition of servitude." Stanton contended that women either should get what they wanted in the amendment or should oppose the amendment. Because of this attitude, other leaders within the women's rights movement distanced themselves from Stanton. Some of these were well-known and talented women with their own following within the movement, including Elizabeth Blackwell, Julia Ward Howe, and Lucy Stone. Each of these leaders supported abolition and women's rights. These leaders favored abolition, even if

Formed in 1869 by Lucy Stone, Julia Ward Howe, and Josephine Ruffin, the American Woman Suffrage Association (AWSA) split from the National Woman Suffrage Association (NWSA) because the latter group was solely concerned with obtaining the right to vote for women. Pictured here is Lucy Stone, who, in addition to her work with the AWSA, is well known for being the first recorded American woman to keep her own last name after she married.

female suffrage was denied. The difference of opinion led to an outright break in the ranks.

In May 1869, Stanton and Anthony founded the National Woman Suffrage Association (NWSA). The

NWSA objected to the Fifteenth Amendment because it contained no guarantees for women's suffrage. Other prominent female leaders, such as Matilda Joslyn Gage and Sojourner Truth (a former slave) joined the NWSA. The disagreement led to a split in female suffrage efforts when six months later Howe, Stone, and Josephine Ruffin formed the American Woman Suffrage Association (AWSA). The

ENGLISH SUFFRAGETTES

The term *suffragette* refers to the women who fought for their right to vote in England in the late nineteenth and early twentieth centuries. Suffragette is derived from *suffrage,* which means "the right to vote." At first, the name was used to describe members of the Women's Social and Political Union (WSPU), a radical and violent splinter group within the English women's suffrage movement. This organization did whatever it could, to draw attention to the issue of female suffrage. Emmeline Pankhurst and her daughter Christabel were leaders of the WSPU, which later advocated violent and illegal acts for the cause. These acts included breaking windows and harassing police officers but later escalated to a decidedly more militant approach, including arson and bombings.

The English authorities took action against the suffragettes for their many violations of various laws by placing them in custody. Once incarcerated, many of the suffragettes refused to eat, choosing instead to resist by participating in self-imposed hunger strikes. The government faced a dilemma: Allow the prisoners to harm themselves and risk the blame, or compel the prisoners to eat. At first, the government chose to force-feed the prisoners, which increased public support for the WSPU. Parliament then passed a law in 1913, nicknamed the Cat and Mouse Act, which provided for the temporary release of hunger-striking prisoners to prevent the death of a suffragette while in jail. Reimprisonments proved difficult, and the impact of the law led to increased sympathy and support for the cause of female suffrage.

One of the most publicized suffragette deeds took place at a horse race in 1913. On that occasion, a suffragette

AWSA argued for ratification of the Fifteenth Amendment, regardless of female exclusion.

In the end, the Fifteenth Amendment passed, winning ratification in February 1870. Unfortunately, the damage to the women's suffrage movement was done. In 1870, there were two major national women's suffrage organizations, and little impetus for change at the national level. Stanton

named Emily Davison went so far as to walk in front of King George V's horse while it was racing at the Epsom Derby. The horse struck and trampled Davidson, who died from her injuries four days later.

American supporters of women's right to vote eventually rejected use of the term *suffragette*, for at least two reasons. First, opponents used "suffragette" as a way to demean and disregard suffrage proponents because it sounded more feminine than suffragist. Second, suffragette became associated with radical militancy, and its use fell out of favor in the United States. Instead, suffrage advocates adopted the preferred and more mainstream term of *suffragist*. This more generic term referred to any supporters of female suffrage, regardless of gender or political affiliation. In England, the two terms signified the differences between the two wings of the suffrage movement; suffragette for the more radical faction, suffragist for the mainstream organization.

During World War I, the WSPU temporarily ceased their protests against the government, choosing instead to support the war effort. The move gained them mainstream approval, but another Pankhurst daughter, Sylvia, then split off to lead the even more militant Women's Suffrage Federation throughout the war. Following the war, Parliament enacted the Representation of the People Act, which allowed women to vote, but included restrictions of age (30), property ownership, and marriage (wives of householders). Agitation continued until 1928, when England finally granted women what English men already enjoyed: the right to vote at age 21.

and the others did not know it, but American women would have to wait another half century before finally winning the right to vote.

A WIDENING RIFT

The ratification of the Fifteenth Amendment did not lessen the tensions between the NWSA and AWSA. Instead, new differences emerged to further drive apart the two organizations. Much of this was caused by Stanton's leadership. She had always held strong beliefs about fundamentalist Christianity, and of the two groups, the AWSA was more conservative, both politically and religiously. Stanton put forward her beliefs in *The Woman's Bible*, a feminist interpretation of the Bible. Specifically, Stanton believed that society, through organized Christianity, consigned women to an inferior place and subservient role. Others, such as Lucretia Mott, disagreed. Mott believed it was not the religion, but rather some individuals within Christianity that created inequality. Stanton, though, could not see the difference, and her commentary on the Bible alienated her from many within the movement.

Although she was a controversial figure, even within the women's rights movement, Elizabeth Cady Stanton continued to contribute to the cause. Utilizing her expertise as a writer, Stanton drafted speeches for herself, Anthony, and others and also penned the text for newspaper articles, pamphlets, and other publications used to communicate the need for social reform. She did not claim all the credit for her writing ability, however; she insisted that her partnership with Susan B. Anthony elevated her writing: "I am the better writer, she the better critic. She supplies the facts and statistics, I the philosophy and rhetoric, and, together, we have made arguments that have stood unshaken through the storms of long years—arguments that no one has answered.

Our speeches may be considered the united product of our two brains."[55] Through her leadership, a women's suffrage amendment proposal earned a spot on the ballot in three states (Kansas, Missouri, and New York) in 1867 and a fourth (Michigan) in 1874. She also fought for and eventually won passage of the Married Women's Property Act, in New York State, which extended property rights for women.[56] She even ran for Congress, something unheard of for a woman in her day. Her 1868 bid, although unsuccessful, helped raise awareness of the question of female suffrage.

Like Carrie Chapman Catt and other suffrage leaders who followed, Stanton was also concerned for women outside the United States. Her daughter Harriot Stanton Blatch, an accomplished feminist, lived in Europe, where she campaigned for women's rights. To aid her daughter, Stanton joined in the effort to establish the International Council of Women in 1888.

In the United States, the rift in the women's rights movement was not without consequences. The disappointment of having come so close to earning the right to vote caused Anthony and others to refocus their efforts almost exclusively on women's suffrage. Prior to the 1869 Equal Rights Association vote, general civil rights was a concern within the women's rights movement. After the 1869 vote, however, although many women leaders still desired civil rights protections, female suffrage became the almost single-minded focal point of women's rights, especially for Susan B. Anthony. Perhaps the granting of suffrage to freed male slaves reinforced the idea that the issue could be won. Regardless of the reason, the women's rights movement now had a champion in Anthony who was dedicated to one goal: guaranteeing women the right to vote.

The Right to Vote

The year was 1872, and it was against the law for American women to vote. The date was November 5, Election Day in the state of New York, where Susan B. Anthony lived in Rochester. On that day, she and several other women did something they had never done before: They voted in an American election. The women were determined to test the law, to see if voting rights existed for women. Anthony's actions and the court case that resulted were aimed at advancing the cause of women's rights. Anthony's decision to enter the polling booth and cast a vote was inspired by a novel concept, generated from suffragist Virginia Minor and her husband, Francis. The idea, which offered the opportunity for a change in the way suffrage was viewed, became known as the New Departure.

THE NEW DEPARTURE

An attorney and husband of a female suffragist living in St. Louis offered the movement a new tact. Francis and Virginia Minor detailed an approach to addressing the issue of female suffrage that claimed women already had the right to vote. The Minors argued that the Fourteenth and Fifteenth amendments applied as much to women as they did to men. The Fourteenth Amendment states,

All persons born or naturalized in the United States, and subject to the jurisdiction thereof, are citizens of the United States and of the State wherein they reside. No State shall make or enforce any law which shall abridge the privileges or immunities of citizens of the United States; nor shall any State deprive any person of life, liberty, or property, without due process of law; nor deny to any person within its jurisdiction the equal protection of the laws.[57]

Further, the Fifteenth Amendment stipulates that the "right of citizens of the United States to vote shall not be denied or abridged by the United States or by any State on account of race, color, or previous condition of servitude."[58] This amendment intended to ensure that citizens could exercise the right to vote, regardless of race, skin color, or prior circumstances, such as slavery. Since women of various races and colors lived in the United States and some women had or had not been slaves, the Minors concluded that the protections of these amendments extended to women, too.

The new departure boosted the spirits of the leadership. The position also opened the door to shifting the argument out of the legislative branch and into the judiciary. Perhaps the issue of women's suffrage could be decided in the courts, where the Constitution took precedence over state laws. The foundation for this new approach rested on how the Constitution was interpreted. Anthony and others now believed they might force the issue by simply assuming that they had the right to vote, rather than asking for it. Prior to the election, Anthony urged women across the United States to go to polls on Election Day and try to vote.

Ever a forerunner, Anthony herself did what she asked others to do. On the Friday before the election, she and her three sisters went to a local barbershop, where citizens could register to vote. Three male election workers sat there, registering voters. Anxiously, the men rejected their request to be registered and reminded them that to do so placed them in jeopardy of a financial penalty. Anthony persisted, however, and offered to pay their fines if it came to that. The men hesitated, while Anthony and her sisters continued to exhort them. Finally, two of the three conceded and entered the names of Susan B. Anthony and several other women into the voter registration books for Rochester, New York. Women were now registered to vote in the 1872 presidential election, which was just four days away.

On Election Day, Susan B. Anthony, together with 14 (some sources claim 15) other women, showed up to vote. At age 52, Anthony was voting in a presidential election for the first time in her life. After casting her vote, she wrote to her friend and fellow women's rights activist Elizabeth Cady Stanton, "Well, I have been & gone & done it!! Positively *voted* the Republican ticket—straight—this A.M. at 7 o'clock and *swore my vote in at that*.[59] Although she had clearly violated existing law, the government delayed taking any action. Anthony and the others made headlines, but their actions seemed to have no other effect. The suffragists had hoped for warrants, arrests, and jail time in order to bring more publicity to their cause. Instead, they cast their votes, and nothing seemed to happen.

At the same time, in St. Louis, the Minors also attempted to force the issue. Virginia tried to register to vote, but the registrar of voters, Reese Happersett, refused to add her name to the rolls. Minor filed suit, seeking damages of $10,000. Virginia's husband, Francis, a practicing lawyer, argued in court that, under the Constitution, states had the power to regulate voting rights, but the document "nowhere gives them the power to prevent" citizens from voting.[60] The Minors lost their case, first in the Circuit Court of St. Louis, then in the Missouri Supreme Court. The couple diligently appealed to the U.S. Supreme Court. In 1874, the Supreme Court unanimously dismissed the case. Speaking for the Court, Chief Justice Morrison R. Waite stated, "the Constitution, when it conferred citizenship, did not necessarily confer the right of suffrage."[61] In short, the Court found that citizenship alone did not necessarily guarantee voting rights, even to men. The need to ratify the Fifteenth Amendment, which ensured voting rights to black men, certainly bolsters this view. For the Minors and other suffragists, the courts did not offer any relief for their situation.

In the meantime, after taking no action against the women for voting for nearly two weeks, a U.S. marshal arrested Anthony and the others on November 18, 1872. The U.S. marshal appeared at her door, bearing a warrant, which charged that Anthony was "a person of the female sex" who did "contrary to the statute of the United States of America . . . knowingly, wrongfully, and unlawfully vote."[62] Finally, Anthony had her chance to stand in defiance of inequality. The marshal, however, was not interested in confrontation.

Instead, the marshal was extremely gracious, informing Anthony that she needed to stop by the office of U.S. Commissioner William C. Storrs to discuss her participation in the recent election. Anthony, however, refused to receive anything less or more than the treatment usually accorded lawbreakers. Anthony adamantly demanded to be placed in handcuffs and arrested. The marshal agreed to take her in for processing, but did not want to create a scene and rebuffed the opportunity to place handcuffs on her. In spite of this, Anthony continued to draw attention to the situation by refusing to pay her fee for the trolley ride. Answering the conductor loudly, Anthony declared "I am traveling at the expense of the government," identifying the marshal as the one responsible for paying for her ride.[63]

Each woman faced criminal charges: They had each voted without a lawful right to vote. Anthony pled not guilty, insisting she had done nothing wrong. Commissioner Storrs found Anthony and the other women guilty of violating a federal statute and placed them in custody. To be released, each was required to post a $500 bail bond. Each of the others, except for Anthony, paid their bail immediately, and the prosecutor made a declaration of *nolle prosequi*, Latin for "we shall no longer prosecute," to the judge. For the other women, the ill effects from this first attempt to exercise their right to vote were over.

Whereas the others paid their bail, Anthony took another course: She and her lawyers filed for a writ of *habeas corpus* (requesting a trial). She hoped to lay the groundwork for a constitutional test case. Henry Selden, one of her attorneys, took the writ application to Albany, where he tried to get the U.S. district judge to issue a writ. The district judge turned down the application and raised Anthony's bail to $1,000.

Anthony still refused to pay, opting for incarceration. Selden, a judge and friend and supporter of Anthony's for many years, could not bear to see her languish in jail. Using his own money, Selden posted bail for Anthony. In so doing, the chance for a constitutional case was lost. If Anthony was not sitting in jail, then a writ of habeas corpus was simply unwarranted. Now there was no chance of the U.S. Supreme Court ever hearing Anthony's case.

THE RULING

The matter of the fine was still undecided, however. Anthony's trial was set for June 17, 1873. The presiding judge was Justice Ward Hunt, who had never before heard or ruled on a federal case. The recent appointee owed his new position to Roscoe Conkling, a powerful New York senator and noted opponent of female suffrage. Conkling was also

New York senator Roscoe Conkling was one of the original drafters of the Fourteenth Amendment, which made blacks citizens of the United States. However, the Republican was a staunch opponent of women's suffrage and went out of his way to deny women equal rights.

a member of the so-called "Stalwarts" of the Republican Party, a faction opposed to civil-service reform. Conkling had used his influence to obtain Hunt a seat on the bench.

VICTORIA CLAFLIN WOODHULL

Whereas Anthony and other women decided to vote in the 1872 election, another female activist chose to do something even more radical: She ran for the highest elected office in America, president of the United States. Victoria Woodhull was born in the small town of Homer, Ohio, in 1838. At the time of her death in England in 1927, she had lived a life filled with achievements, setbacks, and controversy.

Susan B. Anthony and Elizabeth Cady Stanton were divided in their opinions on Victoria Woodhull. Stanton admired Woodhull's candor and revolutionary spirit. Anthony distrusted the firebrand, believing Woodhull's penchant for publicity only served the individual, not the movement. Woodhull attempted to take control of the NWSA in 1872, but Anthony used her power as the association's president to frustrate her efforts. Woodhull elected to find some other group through which to promote herself, eventually finding a warm welcome in the Equal Rights Party.

In 1872, Woodhull decided to run for president. Considering women could not even vote at the time, this was a bold decision. Her platform included demands for a progressive income tax, an eight-hour workday, and a host of social programs. Critics labeled her a fanatical revolutionary and anti-American. She advocated free love (and opposed legal regulation of love relationships, including marriage), labor reforms, and women's rights. After she announced her candidacy, a leading American family, the Beechers, stood opposed to her beliefs. The

Hunt arrived at the trial having already penned his verdict. According to court records, Anthony's attorney attempted to place her on the stand, but the prosecutor objected, claiming that as a woman, "She is not competent as a witness in her own behalf."[64] Justice Hunt agreed, and Anthony was denied the opportunity to speak in court as part of her own defense. After the prosecution and the now-hampered defense rested, Justice Hunt ordered the all-male jury to find Anthony guilty. He did not even release them for deliberations, but

Beechers continued to make personal attacks on her. For a time, she took the abuse silently as the coordinated slanders continued. These smears alleged numerous affairs, witchcraft, and prostitution. Victoria approached Henry Ward Beecher, a well-known supporter of female suffrage, and asked him to intervene on her behalf with his family. He rejected her request, and the attacks persisted.

Woodhull finally decided to fight back, publishing details of the rumored affair between Henry Ward Beecher and a married woman. She did so in the hope that the Beecher family would relent and end their attacks upon her. Woodhull soon learned otherwise, when she was arrested by U.S. marshals for mailing so-called obscene literature. The presidential candidate found herself in jail on Election Day. Initially, public opinion favored the actions against her. Eventually, authorities arrested her on eight different occasions on charges of obscenity and libel. In the end, Victoria Woodhull was acquitted of all charges. She had won her cases in court, but the cost of legal fees and jail time had financially ruined her. She lost almost everything.

Still, the controversial candidate accomplished many firsts in her lifetime. She was the first woman to testify before a congressional committee; the first female stockbroker on Wall Street; and the first female presidential candidate (running as the candidate for the Equal Rights Party, with Frederick Douglass as her running mate, the first time a person of color was as a vice presidential candidate).

instead informed them "the result must be a verdict on your part of guilty, and I therefore direct that you find a verdict of guilty."[65] Selden asked the court clerk to poll the jury, but Judge Hunt denied the request, and then dismissed the jury. The guilty verdict stood.

The court reconvened the next day to consider a defense motion for a new trial and announce the sentencing. The resulting hearing was a farce. Justice Hunt denied the defense request for a new trial. Hunt then asked Anthony if she had anything to say before rendering the sentence. Anthony had waited for this chance to speak her mind to the court. She stood and explained how she had no rights simply because she was a woman. She denounced the legitimacy of a government that subjected individuals to such treatment. Judge Hunt was not amused nor did he care to listen. He informed Anthony that her lawyer had already presented the arguments for her case.

Anthony was far from finished, however. She continued to state "the reasons why sentence cannot, in justice, be pronounced" upon her.[66] She reminded the court that the "denial of my citizen's right to vote is the denial of my right to consent as one of the governed."[67] She continued, arguing that such a denial also constituted "the denial of my right of representation as one of the taxed, the denial of my right to a trial by jury of my peers," and "therefore the denial of my sacred life, liberty, and property."[68] At this point Justice Hunt interrupted, insisting, "The Court cannot allow the prisoner to go on."[69]

Anthony paid no attention to Hunt's words, instead continuing to lecture the court for the injustice of passing sentence against a citizen without the opportunity to voice her own defense. Repeatedly, the judge interjected that she must stop. Repeatedly, Anthony continued to speak her mind. Justice Hunt instructed her to sit down, not once but twice. Unrelenting, she asserted her rights as a citizen, claiming that although she had failed to receive justice or "to get a trial by a jury not of my peers," she asked for "not leniency at your hands but rather the full rigors of the law."[70] At this point, Hunt again began to interrupt her. Anthony stopped talking and sat down. Hunt then instructed her to stand, and said, "The sentence of the Court is that you pay a fine of one hundred dollars and the costs of the prosecution."[71]

Still defiant, Anthony boldly told the judge, "I shall never pay a dollar of your unjust penalty," vowing she would spend "not a penny" toward the fine.[72] She ended her retort by pledging to "earnestly and persistently continue to urge all women to the practical recognition of the old revolutionary maxim, that 'Resistance to tyranny is obedience to God.'"[73] Justice Hunt ordered that the defendant not remain in custody, but be released. Once again, without Anthony in jail, there was no chance for the writ of habeas corpus to be the basis for an appeal. Without unlawful imprisonment, the case lacked the significance needed to reach the Supreme Court. For Susan B. Anthony, death would come before women earned the right to vote. Changes in the Constitution did not extend suffrage to American women until 1920.

MAKING THE CASE FOR SUFFRAGE

For the next 20 years, Anthony and Stanton worked tirelessly for women's suffrage. Stanton wrote speeches and Anthony traveled the country and delivered them. Through their efforts, in 1878, supporters introduced in Congress the first female suffrage amendment to the Constitution. Twelve years later, in 1890, Wyoming became the first state to allow women the right to vote. (However, the year after it became a U.S. territory in 1868, Wyoming had granted women the right to vote.) The many years of difficult labor in the cause of suffrage were beginning to reap benefits in the states. Still, the two leaders wanted to effect change in all of American society. They knew that change needed to be directed at the national government.

The opportunity to directly influence the U.S. government finally came in January 1892. Elizabeth Cady Stanton, Susan B. Anthony, and two other suffrage leaders appeared before the House Judiciary Committee to address the issue of suffrage. The committee warmly greeted the representatives

In 1868, Wyoming became a U.S. territory, and the following year, John A. Campbell, the territory's first governor, signed the "Female Suffrage" bill, which gave women the right to vote. Here, women cast ballots during a local election in the territorial capital of Cheyenne in 1869.

to the hearing. The women were allowed to read from their prepared statements without interruption. Stanton, true to her form and exhibiting her oratory skills, discussed voting rights and the role of women. She powerfully articulated the necessity of rethinking the role of women in society, reminding the committee that each woman is an individual:

> The isolation of every human soul and the necessity of self-dependence must give each individual the right to choose his own surroundings. The strongest reason for giving woman all the opportunities for higher education, for the full development of her faculties, her forces of mind and body; for giving her the most enlarged freedom of thought and action; a complete emancipation from all forms of bondage, of custom, dependence, superstition; from all the crippling influences of fear—is the solitude and personal responsibility of her own individual life. The strongest reason why we ask for woman a voice in the government under which she lives; in the religion she is asked to believe; equality in social life, where she is the chief factor; a place in the trades and professions, where she may earn her bread, is because of her birthright to self-sovereignty; because, as an individual, she must rely on herself.[74]

FAILURE IS IMPOSSIBLE

The long fight finally ended for Elizabeth Cady Stanton. She died on October 26, 1902, at her home in New York City. In the course of her life, tremendous change took place for American women. Her own daughters enjoyed an opportunity she was denied: the chance to attend a formal college. She did not live to see women win the right to vote, but at the time of her death, several states did allow women some voting rights. The battle was over for this reformer, but others continued waging the war on her behalf.

The week of Anthony's eighty-sixth birthday, in 1906, suffragists held celebrations in honor of her and her achievements. Anthony gave her last speech at one of these parties, thanking everyone for the outpouring of support.

Although neither Susan B. Anthony (left) nor Elizabeth Cady Stanton lived to see women gain the right to vote, the work they did to promote women's suffrage was irreplaceable. Here, the two women sit on Anthony's porch at her Rochester, New York, home shortly before Stanton's death in 1902.

She then named many of the inspirational women who had impacted her life: Mary Wollstonecraft (through her writings), Lucretia Mott, the Grimké Sisters, Elizabeth Cady Stanton, and Lucy Stone. She concluded by saying that those individuals and others like them were "a long galaxy of great women. . . . There have been others also just as true to the cause—I wish I could name every one—but with such women consecrating their lives . . . Failure is impossible!"[75]

Less than a month later, on March 13, 1906, Susan B. Anthony died. The suffrage movement lost its two most important and leading figures in the span of just four years. However, Anthony had already handpicked someone to lead the way—Carrie Chapman Catt. Several years before she died, Anthony had remarked of her eventual death and the suffrage movement, wishing others would "go on with the work."[76] Although Catt would step away from the goal of women's suffrage for more than a decade, she did go on with the work, and she eventually provided the vision, leadership, and plan to successfully ensure that women obtained the right to vote.

Carrie Chapman Catt and the Nineteenth Amendment

The Nineteenth Amendment to the U.S. Constitution states (in Section 1) that the right of citizens of the United States to vote shall not be denied or abridged by the United States or by any State on account of sex, and (in Section 2) that Congress shall have power to enforce this article by appropriate legislation.

As simple and as reasonable as the language of that amendment reads, it took more than 40 years from its inception in 1878 to win approval and adoption. Neither Susan B. Anthony, who wrote and drafted the women's suffrage amendment, nor Elizabeth Cady Stanton, who fought for suffrage and other women's rights, lived to see the Nineteenth Amendment win ratification. Instead, another woman, much younger than either Anthony or Stanton, carried on the work, as Stanton knew other women would. Carrie Chapman Catt took up the fight as her own, seeing it through until victory was won.

CARRIE CHAPMAN CATT

Carrie Lane (better known as Carrie Chapman Catt) was born January 9, 1859, in Ripon, Wisconsin. At age seven, she and her family relocated to a small rural community in northern

Iowa, Charles City. Later in life, she once described herself as having been "an ordinary child in an ordinary family on an ordinary farm."[77] There was very little that was ordinary about this woman, however. As a junior in high school, Carrie was already determined to go to college. Her father helped her reach her goal. In 1880, Carrie graduated from Iowa State Agricultural College (now Iowa State University). She was the only woman in a class of 19. The ambitious 21-year-old graduate set her sights on practicing law, as women were gaining acceptance into that line of work.

Instead of law, however, the future national figure began her professional career in one of the few fields open to women: education. She served as a teacher, but her determination and abilities soon landed her an opportunity in administration that few women at the time could have imagined achieving. In March 1883, the local school board promoted Carrie, now 24 years old, to superintendent of schools for Mason City. She was one of the first women in the nation to earn such a position. It was indeed a remarkable accomplishment for a woman in that day and age. Carrie continued to teach as well as perform her administrative duties.

Also in March 1883, a man named Leo Chapman acquired the *Mason City Republican*, the town's weekly newspaper. The new owner served as the paper's editor and became actively involved in the community. Soon, the young teacher and the newspaper editor became friends and then started dating.

MARRIAGE AND THE TRIALS OF LIFE

In a ceremony conducted in her hometown of Charles City, Carrie Lane married Leo Chapman on February 12, 1885. According to the custom of the day, married women were not allowed to teach. Thus, Carrie was forced to give up her position in the school system. She directed her energies to helping her husband with the paper, serving as co-editor of the *Mason City Republican*. Soon the paper reflected her contributions with the inclusion of a new segment entitled "Woman's World." She used the section as a platform to raise awareness of women's issues. In "Woman's World," Carrie Chapman "listed notable achievements of women, wrote articles on a woman's right to strike for better pay and working conditions, published notes of feminist interest from other publications, and reminded readers of the need to work for woman suffrage."[78]

In October 1885, Carrie traveled to Des Moines, where she attended her first women's conference. While there, she became acquainted with some of the leading figures of the women's rights movement. After the conference, Chapman described these women in her "Woman's World" as "the strongest, best educated, most earnest, broad-minded, and philosophical women in the United States."[79] The conference stirred something within Chapman, motivating her and a few others to collect signatures in support of female suffrage. Chapman and the others presented the petition to the Iowa state legislature the following year.

The year 1886 was one of change and tragedy for the newly wedded Chapmans. The two sold the *Mason City Republican* early in the year and made preparations to move to California. Leo went by himself, in search of employment while Carrie remained in Charles City, Iowa, with her parents. In August, Carrie received a distressing telegram: Leo was dreadfully ill with typhoid fever. Carrie quickly left by train for California, but Leo succumbed to the illness while she was en route. Upon arriving in San Francisco, Carrie found herself in a desperate situation. She had little money, her husband was dead, and she had no job. After paying funeral expenses, the young widow did not have the financial means to survive, especially given her desire to advance women's rights.

Carrie decided to remain in San Francisco, where she obtained a job as the city's first female newspaper reporter. While there, she reconnected with George Catt, a wealthy engineer who had been a classmate of hers in college. Catt encouraged her to pursue a speaking career. Carrie welcomed the idea and soon poured her energies into her writing. When she had three well-written and rehearsed lectures, Carrie hired an agent. Then, she began making appearances. While in San Francisco, she delivered and refined her speeches. Equipped for a new career, Carrie returned home to Charles City, Iowa, in 1887. There she worked successfully as a freelance writer and lecturer. She also became a member of the Iowa Woman Suffrage Association (IWSA). Shortly after joining this organization, she became its recording secretary. Later, she served as the organizer for the IWSA.

REMARRIAGE AND SUFFRAGE

In 1890, Carrie Chapman married George Catt, her longtime friend. At the time, Catt served as head of the San Francisco Bridge Company. The two were married on June 10 in Seattle, Washington, where Catt was overseeing the reconstruction of bridges and harbor structures devastated in the Great Seattle Fire of 1889.

The relationship was anything but traditional. This marriage enabled Carrie to dedicate much of her time traveling the country, promoting women's suffrage. She understood that their relationship was unique, but also knew that it worked. Carrie later described her marriage with George Catt this way:

> We made a team to work for the cause. My husband used to say that he was as much a reformer as I, but that he couldn't work at reforming and earn a living at the same time; but what he could do was earn living enough for two

and free me from all economic burden, and thus I could reform for two. That was our bargain and we happily understood each other.[80]

No longer needing to worry about finances, Carrie Chapman Catt was now poised to lead the fight to win women the right to vote. And lead she did.

UNITING FOR SUFFRAGE

In 1890, the women's suffrage movement lacked unity. The movement was divided between the National Woman Suffrage Association (NWSA) and the American Woman Suffrage Association (AWSA). The two organizations shared common roots, but they had divided over objections to the wording in the Fifteenth Amendment, which failed to include women in its guarantees. Leaders within both organizations came to believe that merging the two organizations would focus their efforts and strengthen their chances of success.

One notable leader of the NWSA disagreed with this reasoning because of philosophical objections to AWSA values. Elizabeth Cady Stanton believed that organized religion oppressed women. Her views led her to argue against fusing the NWSA with the religiously conservative AWSA. Her protestations stemmed from the religious and political differences between the two organizations. The spirit of unity prevailed, though, and the two organizations combined in 1890 to become the National American Woman Suffrage Association (NAWSA), in large part attributable to Susan B. Anthony's leadership and persuasiveness. As a testament to Stanton's stature within the movement, and thanks to Anthony's maneuvering, the NAWSA elected Elizabeth Cady Stanton as its first president. Despite the gesture, many women from the former AWSA still distrusted Stanton because of her stance on religion. It would take the

In 1890, the National Woman Suffrage Association (NWSA) and the American Woman Suffrage Association (AWSA) merged to form the National American Woman Suffrage Association (NAWSA). Here, members of the NWSA meet in Washington, D.C., in 1888, shortly before the two groups merged. Among those members pictured here is Elizabeth Cady Stanton (front row, third from right).

leadership of Carrie Chapman Catt to heal those old wounds and ease feelings of mistrust.

CATT RISES TO PROMINENCE

Carrie's marriage to George Catt reaped other benefits, as well. The two temporarily moved to Boston when George needed to manage a building project there. They arrived back East in time for Carrie to attend the annual NAWSA convention in Washington, D.C. While at this gathering, Susan B. Anthony, by then president of the organization, appointed Catt head of a new NAWSA committee charged with recruitment and education of new suffragists. Carrie Chapman Catt now worked for the NAWSA, hiring keynote speakers, making the necessary arrangements, planning trips, raising money, and generally helping promote the cause of women's suffrage. Her talents and experience were now being used for the benefit of the issue that mattered most to her: gaining voting rights for women.

Catt now held a position in which she could try out some of her ideas for advancing female suffrage. Having come from the Midwest, Catt knew that many women in the region supported women's right to vote, but few had the opportunity to attend the national conferences held annually in the nation's capital. To address this deficiency, Catt proposed holding other conferences in places closer to where suffragists lived. In September 1892, she convened a regional gathering, the Mississippi Valley Conference in Des Moines, Iowa. A later tour of the South convinced Catt that some structural changes needed to be implemented if the NAWSA were to grow and achieve reform.

Because of her age, Catt was a relative newcomer to the national women's rights movement. She quickly ascended to positions of leadership. Her speaking and organizational skills were a natural fit for leading a movement that often lacked the funds to carry out their tasks. In time, Catt and Susan B. Anthony developed a strong working relationship. It was Anthony who designated Catt as her successor as president of the NAWSA. Catt served from 1900 to 1904 and effectively led or strongly influenced the leadership of the NAWSA for more than 20 years.

Relying on her experiences in Iowa, Catt utilized sound planning and well-orchestrated public events to advance the cause of female suffrage. Her ability to coordinate large groups of volunteer help was unparalleled in the women's rights movement. At the height of the battle for ratification of the Nineteenth Amendment, Catt oversaw the planning and implementation of campaign details for one million volunteers, all without the assistance of modern technology!

INTERNATIONAL FEMALE SUFFRAGE

After being elected president of the NAWSA, Catt supported efforts to establish an international organization dedicated to promoting female suffrage throughout the world. Such an organization already existed, the International Council of Women (ICW). Yet, the ICW also supported other issues that were not solely women's issues, such as improving education, world peace, sanitation, and so on. Catt did not believe that women's suffrage received the kind of focused attention needed to win reform.

Catt again proved her mastery at organization and coordination. In advance of the first international gathering, Catt contacted leaders in many different nations by sending out a questionnaire. Delegates from 32 countries sent responses. Through these questionnaires, Catt collected and organized the information about women's rights throughout the world. The results confirmed that women in various countries lacked basic political and legal rights, simply because they were women.

Armed with her survey results, Catt now had the rationale for creating an international group to promote women's suffrage. On February 12, 1902, Catt founded the International Woman Suffrage Alliance (IWSA). Suffragists from 11 countries outside the United States attended the initial conference, which was held in conjunction with the annual NAWSA convention in Washington, D.C. At the time, eight countries had organizations dedicated to achieving female suffrage; seven of those sent representatives to the inaugural IWSA meeting (the United States, Sweden, Norway, Great Britain, Germany, Denmark, and Australia). Others came from Switzerland, Turkey, Russia, Hungary, and Chile. After the initial meeting, interest in international women's suffrage continued to grow. Soon, Carrie Chapman Catt found that devoting her time to both organizations was spreading her thin. The IWSA now took more and more of Catt's time. Consequently, Catt resigned her post as president of the NAWSA in 1904 in order to concentrate exclusively on promoting international women's rights and to care for her husband, whose health was failing.

George Catt died in 1905, and Carrie Chapman Catt then dedicated her time and strength to both local and international organizations concerned with women's rights. These organizations included city and state suffrage groups in New York, as well as the International Woman Suffrage Alliance. She served as president of the latter organization until 1923. Her efforts in two campaigns, beginning in 1912 in New York State, resulted in a 1914 legislative act recognizing women's voting rights. Since New York was the largest state by population, this was indeed a tremendous victory for the cause of women's suffrage.

The women's suffrage movement received another boost when the Progressive Party (Bull Moose Party), which nominated former President Theodore Roosevelt as its presidential candidate in 1912, included a plank in its platform supporting the passage of a constitutional amendment guaranteeing female suffrage. Roosevelt and the Progressives failed to win the election, but that issue was gaining prominence. The Bull Moose Party fell into obscurity, but both the Democrat and Republican parties took up support for female suffrage, adding language to their party platforms. The suffragists now had the backing of both major parties, raising the chances of success.

THE WINNING PLAN

The women's rights movement's eventual victory in gaining the right to vote was attributable in large part to Carrie Chapman Catt. Her dedication, vision, and determination to

During her time as president of the NAWSA, Carrie Chapman Catt mobilized approximately one million volunteers and made hundreds of speeches supporting women's suffrage. Catt and former NAWSA president Dr. Anna Howard Shaw are pictured here leading women's suffrage supporters in a march down New York's Fifth Avenue in 1915.

continue the fight for political equality finally culminated in success during her second term as president of the NAWSA. When Anna Howard Shaw resigned as president of the NAWSA in 1915, Carrie Chapman Catt seemed the obvious choice. She had already served as president of the association and her abilities as an organizer were unquestioned. Catt was reluctant to step forward, however, fearful that such a commitment would hinder her efforts with the IWSA. After weighing the situation, Catt agreed to serve a second term as president of the NAWSA.

Catt energetically set out to redefine and refocus the association. First, she traveled to a large number of suffrage events: local meetings, state conventions, regional conferences, virtually anywhere that suffragists might be. She familiarized herself with the leaders of the movement and also let the workers and state representatives get to know her. Satisfied that she understood the progress made by the movement's leaders since she last served as president, Catt then called for a summit with all the presidents of the state organizations. At this gathering, Catt demonstrated her ability to organize and focus the movement's energies. The president unveiled a new approach to winning suffrage. The plan was bold, but it was also clear and easy to understand. Catt's vision became known as the "Winning Plan," although Catt herself referred to it as a "new deal."[81] The Winning Plan consisted of four major steps to obtaining suffrage.

1. Convince each state legislature to pass resolutions to Congress in support of female suffrage.

2. Organize and campaign for referendums on constitutional amendments granting female suffrage in various states.

3. Petition "each state to give women whatever suffrage they could, preferably rights to vote in presidential elections."[82]

4. Promote voting rights in primary elections.

Catt's strategy allowed for local and state participation, but still increased pressure at the national level. In short, this line of attack ensured that every political official—local, state, or national—had to address the issue. Volunteers pressured virtually every politician in the country to declare his stand on women's suffrage. Catt's intensity emanated from her belief in a woman's equality with men and her natural right to take part in the political process. Without suffrage, women suffered indignities at the hands of those individuals who held political power. Suffrage would arm women with influence over elected officials. Catt also strongly believed that women's participation in the political arena would serve to improve the world by protecting the rights of women and children domestically and promoting peace abroad.

SUFFRAGE ABOVE ALL OTHER PRINCIPLES

In addition to suffrage rights for women, Carrie Chapman Catt also believed in and promoted the idea of world peace. When the United States entered World War I, Catt remained focused on her overriding goal of winning suffrage. Despite her pacifism, Catt encouraged American suffragists to continue to work within the system in order to win the right to vote. If there was some aspect of government action they could support, then they should support the war effort. She stated, "I am myself a pacifist, now and forever. War to my mind is a barbarism, but I hold that that belief has nothing to do with the present situation. Whether we approve or disapprove, war is here. It is not the appeal of war, but the call of civilization which is summoning women to new duties and responsibilities."[83]

Catt's example opened the door for suffragists to be active supporters of the war effort, even if only in displays of humanitarianism. Catt did not allow the suffrage movement to become distracted with the issue of pacifism. This short-term concession reaped enormous dividends. Such actions allowed the NAWSA to escape public scorn for being unpatriotic.

Even during the war, Catt's leadership and Winning Plan began to bear fruit. North Dakota approved a measure allowing women to vote in municipal and presidential elections in January 1917. The next month, Ohio extended to women the right to vote in presidential elections. Arkansas granted women's suffrage in primaries that March. Moreover, in April, Rhode Island, Nebraska, and Michigan extended the right to vote to women for presidential elections. Momentum now favored the suffragists.

Despite these accomplishments, the leadership within the National American Women Suffrage Association soon

JEANNETTE RANKIN: THE FIRST FEMALE MEMBER OF CONGRESS

In 1916, Jeannette Pickering Rankin became the first woman to be elected to the U.S. House of Representatives, four years before most American women even had the right to vote. Rankin, a native of Montana, graduated from the University of Montana in 1902. Later, she attended graduate school in New York City and took a job as a social worker in Seattle. In 1910, she became actively involved in the cause of women's suffrage.

On March 4, 1917, the new Congress was sworn into office. For the first time in America's history, there was a female member of Congress. The first challenging vote to face Rankin came just weeks later, on April 6, when the House voted on President Woodrow Wilson's request for a declaration of war against Germany. Rankin, a declared pacifist, had promised in her campaign to help keep the United States out of the great conflict. She was hardly alone on this stand during the campaign; even President Wilson assured supporters before the election that he intended to keep the country out of the war. However, the political climate changed between the November election and the swearing in of the new Congress. First, Germany announced and began again to utilize its great fleet of submarines against all Allied ships, even passenger ships. Second, the publication of the Zimmerman Telegram detailed Germany's attempt to persuade Mexico to attack the United States. Together, these two issues helped create widespread public support for the war.

By the time Rankin took office, American sentiment favored war with Germany. Leading suffragists, including Carrie Chapman Catt, pressured Rankin to vote for the

began to fracture. Carrie Chapman Catt advocated an approach in which the suffragists supported individuals and policy makers for public office in the hope and expectation of gaining political allies. To achieve this, Chapman Catt war, in order to prevent harm to the cause of suffrage. Catt argued that voting against the war effort would mean almost certain defeat for Rankin in the next election. The more radical Alice Paul, like Rankin a pacifist, advised the representative "to vote her conscience regardless of the consequences."* The new Montana representative remained true to her campaign pledge. Rankin and 49 other House members voted against the declaration of war. The measure passed easily without their support, and the United States entered World War I.

As Catt had predicted, the vote cost Rankin support. She did not seek reelection to the House in 1918 but tried unsuccessfully to run for the Senate. For the next 20 years, Rankin worked as a lobbyist, serving as the founding vice president of the American Civil Liberties Union (ACLU) and a founding member of the Women's International League for Peace and Freedom. She again ran as a pacifist for a congressional seat in 1940, winning that election. She took her seat in January 1941. By the end of the year, however, she faced yet another vote on a declaration of war, this time the day after Japan attacked Pearl Harbor. Once again, Rankin voted her conscience, casting the only Congressional vote against U.S. entry into World War II. She did not seek reelection in 1942 but continued to work as a peace activist until her death in Carmel, California, on May 18, 1973. In 1975, a statue of Rankin was added to the U.S. Capitol's Statuary Hall.

---

* Christine A. Lunardini, *Women's Rights* (Phoenix, Ariz.: Oryx Press, 1996), 105.

worked tirelessly in support of President Woodrow Wilson, a progressive Democrat who was reelected in 1916. She also publicly backed the president when the United States entered World War I.

THE SILENT SENTINELS

To mount an even greater political threat, two of the more radical suffrage leaders, Alice Paul and Lucy Burns, co-founded a new organization. This organization was initially called the Congressional Union for Woman Suffrage. The group later changed its name to the National Woman's Party (NWP). Paul and this group espoused a more radical approach to the question of women's rights, going so far as to prohibit men from joining the organization. The NWP split off from the NAWSA in 1913, largely in defiance of the association's conciliatory approach to elected officials. At the initial meeting, Alice Paul explicitly stated this point, promising that the NWP would not name nor endorse a candidate campaigning for office. Instead, the National Woman's Party was intended to be nonpartisan.

Alice Paul and the NWP largely ignored state governments, instead focusing their efforts on convincing Congress to pass a constitutional amendment guaranteeing women's right to vote. The NWP gained national attention when Paul and many other members appeared in Washington, D.C., to stage a protest the day before President Wilson took office. Police dispersed protesters, and many of the participants wound up in jail. Several members of the NWP resorted to a hunger strike to protest their incarceration. Authorities responded by force-feeding some of the women. The ensuing media coverage resulted in public outrage at home, and Woodrow Wilson was forced to deflect international criticism. Ironically, Wilson seemed intent on establishing himself as a champion of human rights on the world stage. Perhaps the embarrassment of such shameful acts within the United States finally led the president to challenge Congress to pass the Nineteenth Amendment for the states to consider for ratification.

Alice Paul and the NWP picketed the White House throughout Wilson's presidency, even during World War I. These "Silent Sentinels" protested Wilson by staging pickets six days a week for more than two and a half years. Whereas Catt and the NAWSA desired to work with whomever held office, the NWP intended to exert pressure on whomever was in power, especially by raising public awareness and staging embarrassing scenes of picketers and parades. When the United States entered World War I, the pacifist NWP angrily objected. President Wilson now represented two great evils to the NWP: He was a wartime president and his administration had not advanced suffrage. As such, Wilson received a great deal of the group's indignation.

The differing tactics of the NAWSA and the NWP each had their strengths, but the two organizations continued to diverge. Both groups concentrated their efforts on winning suffrage, but they did not seem open to working with or for racial equality. Whereas the abolitionists had abandoned women's rights in the 1860s, the women's rights movement seemed willing to abandon African Americans in the 1910s.

The dual strategies of the two competing organizations worked; President Wilson recognized the contributions of women to the war effort, and he tired of the constant picketing. As Catt had hoped, support for the war resulted in a change of heart in the president. Wilson declared his support for the Nineteenth Amendment by stating, "The services of women during the supreme crisis have been the most signal usefulness. . . . It is high time that part of our debt should be acknowledged and paid."[84] Indeed, the time had come, and Congress finally addressed the issue that so many states had already tackled. Wilson also affirmed his support for suffrage in a September 1918 speech. He stated. "We have made partners of the women in this war. Shall we admit them only to a partnership of suffering and sacrifice and toil and not to a partnership of right?"[85]

The election of 1918 shifted the balance of power for the issue of women's suffrage. This time the House overwhelmingly voted in favor of the amendment, 304 to 89 on May 21, 1919. The U.S. Senate followed suit just 15 days later, giving approval by a 56 to 25 vote. Now the battleground shifted to the states, where legislatures weighed whether or not to ratify the amendment. Within just 14 months, 35 of the 36 necessary states had already ratified the amendment. Victory was within reach.

VICTORY AT LAST

Catt and the suffragists now lacked just one state to achieve their long-sought goal of political equality. Several states that did not ratify the amendment remained strongly opposed to ratification. Many of these states were in the South. The chance to win ratification still existed in Tennessee, however. Tensions and excitement reached a peak in July 1920, when the Tennessee House voted on the issue. What appeared to be a 48–48 tie was broken when 24-year-old Harry Burn took the advice of his mother, a suffragist. In his pocket he had a letter in which his mother exhorted him, "Don't forget to be a good boy" and "vote for suffrage."[86] Twice that day, Harry Burn had called out an "Aye" vote, although each of those votes were in support of tabling the resolution. When the clerk called his name for the third time that day, Harry Burn again called out an "Aye" vote. This time, it was a vote for suffrage. This time, it was the deciding vote. Later, Harry explained his decision, "I know that a mother's advice is always safest for a boy to follow."[87]

As soon as Burn cast his vote, the suffragists realized the amendment would pass. Suffrage supporters were unable to contain their excitement. The cries, applause, and shouts

On August 18, 1920, Harry Burn cast the deciding vote in the Tennessee Legislature's special session to decide whether or not to pass the Nineteenth Amendment. From that point forward, women could cast their ballots in both local and national elections. Here, Carrie Chapman Catt and Mary Garrett Hay hand over their ballots during the 1920 presidential election at a polling station in New York City.

of anger and jubilation were so loud that it "was heard for blocks around the Capitol."[88] Burn proved to be a good boy and voted as his mother wished. The result was the ratification of the Nineteenth Amendment. The long wait was finally over. Female suffrage was now a reality. American women now had the right to vote.

9

The Equal Rights Amendment

After the Nineteenth Amendment won ratification, Alice Paul took up another fight for women, one in which she sought to end all forms of sexual and gender discrimination. Paul drafted the Equal Rights Amendment and began to promote its adoption. The National Woman's Party (NWP) also began publication of *Equal Rights*, a magazine dedicated to educating American women and men on subjects such as women's rights, the advantages of female suffrage, and a host of other topics related to women.

Not all suffragists agreed with the strategy of the NWP. As in the 1860s, tensions rose between activists who supported the single issue of suffrage and those who supported a host of other issues. In the 1910s and 1920s, several prominent feminists, such as Jane Addams, Florence Kelley, and Rose Schneiderman, each spoke out against the NWP's policy of focusing on equal rights for women. As an alternative, these women supported much broader reforms, such as the progressive and labor movements. Such groups advocated reforms that indirectly benefited women. Addams was an activist of the Women's Trade Union League, which had successfully fought for the passage of laws designed to limit working hours for women and ensure minimum wages. Many of these women were especially opposed to the Equal Rights Amendment because of earlier legislative victories that offered protections for female workers. In any case, the NWP and its radicalism turned off enough women that the group soon became ineffective. As other groups became more established, the influence of the NWP diminished to the point that, just 10 years after the Nineteenth Amendment was ratified, it was no longer the premier women's organization.

UNFINISHED BUSINESS

The 1920 ratification of the Nineteenth Amendment was accomplished through many years of hard work. The battle for the right to vote had begun in the United States 80 years earlier and was achieved 72 years after the women's rights convention in Seneca Falls, New York. After ratification, however, at least one reformer, Alice Paul, was not satisfied. In 1921, she drafted the text of what later became known as the Equal Rights Amendment (ERA). It was simple and to the point:

> SECTION 1. Equality of rights under the law shall not be denied or abridged by the United States or by any State on account of sex.
>
> SECTION 2. The Congress shall have the power to enforce, by appropriate legislation, the provisions of this article.
>
> SECTION 3. This amendment shall take effect two years after the date of ratification.

Alice Paul maintained that voting rights alone did not provide sufficient protections from sexual discrimination imbedded throughout American legal codes. Paul composed the ERA to address these issues. In 1923, she introduced it as the Lucretia Mott Amendment, in honor of the 1848 Seneca Falls Declaration of Sentiments, delivered 75 years earlier. From there, the National Woman's Party convinced two Republicans from Kansas to submit it to Congress for

(continues on page 116)

LEAGUE OF WOMEN VOTERS

In 1919, the National American Woman Suffrage Association (NAWSA) met for their final convention and stood on the verge of achieving victory for women's suffrage with the passage of the Nineteenth Amendment in Congress. The NAWSA believed that both the House and Senate would support the amendment. Once the amendment passed, the NAWSA would no longer be needed. Carrie Chapman Catt, president of the NAWSA, encouraged the delegates present to consider forming a new organization. This new group was to help educate American women who now had the right to vote. Catt wanted to ensure women were prepared to be responsible citizens and voters.

According to author Christine A. Lunardini, Catt offered a vision for the new organization, consisting of three main objectives. First, the organization needed to ensure that the women's suffrage amendment was ratified by the necessary number of states. Second, it was essential for the group "to take the lead in eliminating any remaining discrimination against women."* Finally, the new organization needed to take steps to ensure American democracy was sound, in order for the United States to defend world security. Catt's arguments swayed enough members of the NAWSA that they established the League of Women Voters (LWV) in 1920. The member honored Catt and her work for female suffrage by naming her president for life, although it was another longtime NAWSA member, Maud Wood Park, who served as the league's first president.

The LWV sought to influence policy on 38 different legislative acts in the 1920s. The group claimed victory only twice in that decade, however. The first success came in 1921 with the passage of the Sheppard-Towner Act, which offered medical care to women and children. The second came in 1922, when Congress enacted the Cable Citizenship Act, which protected the citizenship rights of women married to noncitizens.

Initially, the LWV only allowed women to enlist as members. However, the charter was amended in 1973 to allow men into the League as well. In 2006, the LWV boasted a membership of about 150,000, with chapters in every state, Washington, D.C., the U.S. Virgin Islands, and Puerto Rico.

Instead of endorsing specific candidates or parties, the league is a nonpartisan organization. Thus, the LWV promotes or counters stances on issues rather than candidates. Its primary focus is to raise awareness and build support for key policy issues facing Americans. Relying on education and lobbying, the LWV attempts to shape policy at all levels of government.

The LWV sponsored the presidential debates in 1976, 1980, and 1984. Controversy arose in 1988, however, when both the Democratic and Republican parties insisted on controlling details of the debates, such as how they would be conducted, where they would be held, how many there would be, and so on. The LWV protested the parties' control over the debates and pulled out on October 3, 1988, declaring their belief that "the demands of the two campaign organizations would perpetrate a fraud on the American voter" and the debates would simply be added to the "list of campaign-trail charades devoid of substance, spontaneity and answers to tough questions."[**] The LWV maintained its intention of not "becoming an accessory to the hoodwinking of the American public."[***] The two major parties formed the Commission on Presidential Debates, which now acts as the sponsor for all presidential debates.

Today, the LWV still sponsors debates and acts a moderator for candidates in state and local elections. During election campaigns, the LWV also publishes voter's guides listing the candidates' stands on a range of issues. In some precincts, local chapters of the organization help in the democratic process by providing volunteers to help run elections. Much as Catt envisioned, the League of Women Voters is an organization that continues to educate voters and encourage the electoral process.

---

[*] Christine A. Lunardini, *Women's Rights* (Phoenix, Ariz.: Oryx Press, 1996), 103.

[**] "Revealing History: Strengthens the Major Parties." Available online at *http://www.opendebates.org/theissue/ strengthenmajorparties.html*

[***] Ibid.

Despite gaining the right to vote in 1920, the Nineteenth Amendment did not protect women from sexual discrimination. To help address this issue Alice Paul and Lucy Burns founded the National Woman's Party (NWP) in 1913. Eight years later, Paul would draft the Equal Rights Amendment (ERA), which has yet to be adopted into law. Paul (second from right) is pictured here with (left to right) Sue White, Benigna Green Kalb, Mrs. James Rector, Mary Dubrow, and Elizabeth Kalb at the Republican National Convention in 1920.

(continued from page 113)

consideration in December 1913. Daniel R. Anthony Jr. introduced the measure to the House of Representatives, whereas Charles Curtis did the same in the Senate.

The measures failed to pass, but supporters did not give up, despite facing many years of disappointment. From 1923 to 1970, the ERA was introduced in every session of Congress. The measure seldom even made it out of committee, meaning neither chamber voted on the issue, except in rare cases. The Senate voted down the amendment in 1946 and passed a modified version four years later. Unfortunately, this version, which eliminated all laws that would protect women, did not satisfy those advocates who supported the ERA.

Several groups and prominent Americans strongly contested the ERA. Eleanor Roosevelt, a reputable feminist in her own right, did not believe women should be forced into competition with men in the labor force. Organized labor, led by the American Federation of Labor (AFL), also opposed the ERA. Many others who supported the expansion of government during President Franklin Roosevelt's administration, the so-called New Dealers, were inclined to support government programs to help women rather than those initiatives that ensured female equality.

Finally, after several decades, a Democratic representative from Michigan, Martha W. Griffiths, sponsored the amendment in the House of Representatives. In October 1971, the House passed the measure, 354 to 24, with 51 abstaining. The following March, the Senate passed the amendment, 84 to 8, with 7 abstentions. When the 92nd Congress passed the ERA on to the states for their consideration, they placed a time limit on ratification, continuing the practice first used by Congress in 1917, when it passed the Eighteenth Amendment establishing Prohibition. Now the state legislatures considered the Equal Rights Amendment. To win adoption to the Constitution, 38 states needed to ratify the amendment before March 22, 1979. The ratification fight began in earnest, and it proved to be one of the most contentious in U.S. history.

FIGHTING FOR RATIFICATION

At first, the ERA met considerable success in the state legislatures, with 22 states ratifying the amendment in

1972. Eight more states passed the ERA the following year. Nevertheless, supporters gained victory in only five more states during the next five years, bringing the total number of state ratifications to 35—3 short of the necessary three-fourths majority.

After initially enjoying widespread support and relatively easy legislative victories, momentum for the ERA began to stall. There are several reasons why states hesitated to support the amendment, which would contribute to its eventual defeat. These reasons include the rise of organized opposition, the loss of Republican support, a landmark court case, and a constitutional crisis. Each of these influenced the debate and its outcome.

At the time Congress passed the ERA to the states for ratification, there was little opposition and certainly none that was well organized. That soon changed when prominent antifeminist and conservative political activist Phyllis Schlafly founded an organization in late 1972 called the Eagle Forum. Schlafly and the Eagle Forum are best known as the driving force behind the "Stop ERA" movement. Schlafly used her monthly newsletter, *The Phyllis Schlafly Report*, to detail arguments against the Equal Rights Amendment. Schlafly, perhaps more than any other person, was responsible for defeating the ERA. The conservative activist successfully linked the abortion and gay-rights issues with the ERA, all but ensuring it would be defeated due to the general lack of support for the aforementioned issues.

In 1980, the GOP (Republication Party) voted to end its support for the ERA. Prior to this, the amendment had transcended the two major parties; the ERA had become a partisan issue. In terms of strategy, the ERA now aligned itself almost exclusively with the Democratic Party, thereby risking alienation of possible supporters in the Republican Party.

Another blow to the ERA came when the U.S. Supreme Court released a decision in January 1973 that radically transformed the ERA debate, resurrecting and highlighting old tensions within the movement: *Roe v. Wade*. Prior to the *Roe v. Wade* decision, which legalized abortion, the ERA debate centered on "women's equality vis-à-vis men, and women's consequent need for legal protection."[89] This support for the ERA rested on the premise that the Constitution should offer safeguards to protect women in the same way that men enjoyed legal protections. The amendment was needed, supporters of the ERA argued, because the courts had not afforded women these protections. An amendment to the Constitution would secure the desired protections.

Because of the *Roe v. Wade* decision, however, the debate now included abortion. Some ERA opponents had argued earlier that the ERA would make it easier to get abortions. Because of the *Roe v. Wade* ruling, "advocates believed a major sanction against women's rights had been lifted."[90] In essence, the ruling served to increase the intensity of the debate, as abortion supporters tended to support the ERA, whereas abortion opponents tended to oppose the ERA. With the *Roe v. Wade* decision, opponents of the ERA had a highly visible issue that resonated with many Americans. As opposition to the ERA rose, support for ratification fell.

Finally, a growing constitutional crisis elevated the stature of a U.S. senator and leading opponent of the ERA. When the Senate passed the ERA 84–8 in March 1972, it appeared that public and political support now favored ratification. Senator Sam Ervin Jr. of North Carolina was one of the eight Senators who voted against the measure. Some depicted Ervin as "a persistent and articulate opponent of federal legislation and administrative action that, in his opinion, violated constitutional freedoms."[91] At age 75, Ervin projected the image of an old Southern conservative who simply refused to change with the times.

Despite his image, it was Ervin who had raised the most serious constitutional objection to the wording of the amendment prior to its passage. Ervin believed the ERA was too vaguely worded, opening the door for many future conflicts. Such ambiguity posed threats to the Constitution. In 1970, Ervin argued, "The word 'sex' is imprecise in exact meaning, and no proposed constitutional amendment ever drafted exceeds the House-passed equal rights amendment in scrimpiness of context. The amendment contains no language to elucidate its meaning to legislators or to guide courts in interpreting it."[92] According to Ervin, such wording needed clarity to guide the courts as they applied the amendment to specific cases. Because the ERA lacked such specificity, Ervin remained an outspoken critic of the amendment.

Ervin also asserted the ERA would require women to be drafted and sent into combat, "where they will be slaughtered or maimed by the bayonets, the bombs, the bullets, the grenades, the mines, the napalm, the poison gas, or the shells of the enemy."[93] His arguments helped sway the vote in 1970 and 1971. Moreover, his claims that the ERA would mean that American women would be compelled to serve in the U.S. armed forces reappeared throughout the ratification fight. Nevertheless, Ervin found himself in the minority when Congress again voted on the amendment in 1972.

In May 1973, something dramatic occurred, changing the political landscape and Sam Ervin's persona: the Watergate scandal. Ervin chaired the suddenly important Senate Select Committee on Presidential Campaign Activities (or the Watergate Committee). As chair, Ervin became a household name and national figure. During the Watergate scandal, Ervin's stature grew. The same individuals who had described him as strongly opposed to the ERA in 1972, now portrayed him as defender of the Constitution, writing, "because of his devotion to the Constitution," Ervin "has become a legendary man."[94] Ervin was now considered a constitutional expert. His views on the ERA mattered and could not be ignored. Had the ERA won ratification, Ervin's continued opposition would scarcely have mattered. Nevertheless, the amendment did not win ratification, and supporters were forced to again petition Congress for consideration of their measure.

THE PIVOTAL YEAR: 1975

ERA supporters optimistically predicted victory for the amendment in 1975. Instead, 1975 proved to be "a year of disaster" for the ERA.[95] In January 1975, 33 states had already ratified the ERA. Twelve months later, however, advocates had managed only a single win when North Dakota approved the amendment. Worse still were the referendums that failed in New York and New Jersey, two states that had already ratified the ERA in 1972. Voters rejected equal rights amendments to their state constitutions. The state amendments were described as a way to ensure women's rights until the ERA won ratification. At the crucial moment, New York and New Jersey left supporters of the ERA to fend for themselves. Phyllis Schlafly offered an explanation, claiming the votes signaled a shift in public opinion with "the momentum all against the ERA."[96]

Support for the ERA continued to wane. The Republican Party included a plank in its national platform supporting the ERA in 1972 and again in 1976. However, the 1980 platform stated, "We affirm our Party's historic commitment to equal rights and equality for women."[97] Thus, the GOP, after openly supporting the ERA in two prior presidential elections, seemingly withdrew its support. This retreat

National Rally for Equal Rights

By 1975, 33 states had ratified the Equal Rights Amendment, and it seemed likely that it would finally become law. Unfortunately, for ERA supporters over the next year, only one state, North Dakota, ratified the amendment, and the ERA seemed to have lost its momentum. Here, ERA supporters march on the Illinois capitol building in Springfield to support passage of the amendment in May 1976.

was attributable in part to the controversy surrounding the deadline extension.

DEADLINE CONTROVERSY

Supporters waited nearly 50 years from the initial proposal to congressional approval for the Equal Rights Amendment to be presented to the states for ratification. Immediately after the congressional vote, prospects for the ERA were good. The 1979 deadline loomed ever closer, though, and the amendment still lacked the support of three states. Supporters grew anxious, and in 1978, Elizabeth Holtzman, a member of the House from New York, proposed an extension of the ratification deadline to June 30, 1982. To counter this proposal, opponents called Sam Ervin, now retired, back to Congress to testify against the ERA. He now did so as a constitutional expert, and he again explained his view that vague wording weakened the Constitution. Despite the objections of Ervin and others, however, the extension, contained in a joint resolution approved by both the House and Senate, added an additional three years and three months to the original deadline. The extension only served to cloud the issues, though, and Ervin's testimony helped fuel the debate for opponents of the amendment.

The delay was intended to allow more time for supporters to win approval in three more states, thereby gaining ratification. Nevertheless, the additional time also kept the issue alive in some of the 35 states that had already ratified the amendment. Four of these states—Nebraska, Tennessee, Idaho, and Kentucky—decided to rescind their ratification of the ERA. In addition to these four states, South Dakota voted to retain its support, but only for the period originally set by Congress. Thus, South Dakota's support for the amendment would last only until March 22, 1979. South Dakota maintained that after that date, its vote for the ERA was no longer binding.

Predictably, such actions led to more debate. Some scholars argue that once a state legislature ratifies an amendment to the U.S. Constitution, it cannot then repeal its approval later. Proponents of this view cite ratification of the Fourteenth Amendment in 1868. Two states retracted their affirmation of that amendment prior to the necessary approval from three-fourths of the state legislatures. In that instance, Secretary of State William Seward certified the Fourteenth Amendment as valid, pending resolution of the repeal issue. The very next day, July 21, 1868, Congress voted to accept the amendment. In fact, the Fourteenth Amendment became part of the Constitution, although the issue is still debated among legal scholars today. Thus, past actions indicate the issue belongs in the national legislature, not the courts.

Almost inevitably, all of these political maneuverings led to legal fights. A legal challenge to the congressional extension resulted in a controversial ruling from a U.S. District Court in late 1981. In *State of Idaho et al. v. Freeman et al.*, the federal court ruled that a state could rescind its approval of an unratified amendment. The ruling also stated that the three-plus-year extension of the ERA deadline was unconstitutional. The U.S. Supreme Court, hearing the case on appeal, dismissed it as "moot" in early October 1982. The high court found that because the revised deadline had already passed without the ERA gaining the approval of three more states, further legal proceedings would not affect the situation. The Supreme Court did not address the issue of whether or not the deadline extension was legitimate. Thus, that issue continues to be unresolved.

Despite the extra time, no other state approved the ERA. Instead, both the March 22, 1979, and June 30, 1982 deadline dates passed with much fanfare but no additional state ratifications. The Equal Rights Amendment, first conceived by Alice Paul more than 60 years earlier, appeared to be dead.

10

Women's Rights Today

A mazingly, the ERA debate continues today. Some advocates of the ERA contend that the 35-state ratifications from the 1970s are still legally binding. Under this argument, Congress does not have to pass a new amendment by a two-thirds majority and then propose that amendment to the states for ratification. Instead, these supporters speculate that if three more states ratify the ERA, then the amendment will become part of the U.S. Constitution.

There is some historical precedent for such a scenario. The Twenty-seventh Amendment received final ratification in 1992, more than 200 years after its initial proposal by James Madison in Congress in 1789. The unique path to adoption for this amendment also included a reassertion by the legislative branch that certification of amendments is a congressional power, not a judicial one. Despite the curious means by which it won ratification, the Twenty-seventh Amendment is indeed part of the U.S. Constitution. The U.S. Supreme Court ruled in *Coleman v. Miller* (1939) that amendments to the Constitution were political, not legal, matters. Thus, Congress is the final arbiter of such matters, because amendments must begin with congressional approval and end with congressional certification. In other words, no amendment is valid until Congress says it is, nor is any amendment invalid until Congress says it is.

In the 1997 article "Why the ERA Remains Legally Viable and Properly Before the States," the authors argue several main points in espousing the idea that the ERA could still be ratified. First, the 1970s ratifications by 35 states are still binding. Second, repeals of earlier ratifications are unconstitutional (meaning the original ratifications are still valid). Third, Congress's decision to extend the deadline to 1982 shows that the legislative branch has the power and authority to revise deadlines set previously. Finally, because the Twenty-seventh Amendment took more than two centuries to win ratification, the criteria for congressional deadlines are at the discretion of Congress. If these legal arguments are legitimate, then the ERA might win approval by following the "three-state strategy."[98]

Once again, the Twenty-seventh Amendment gives hope to supporters of the ERA and the three-state strategy. Article V of the U.S. Constitution empowers Congress to propose an amendment and determine the mode of ratification. Article V, however, "is silent as to the power of Congress to impose time limits" on the ratification process.[99]

Two court cases also provide some insight. In *Dillon v. Gloss* (1921), the Supreme Court ruled that Congress has the authority to set a deadline for ratification. The Supreme Court also stated, however, that once an amendment receives approval from three-fourths of the state legislatures, said amendment becomes part of the Constitution. Thus, Congress still serves as the final authority as to whether an amendment is valid.

Nevertheless, in the same case, the Supreme Court also ruled that the Constitution did not seem to permit "that an amendment once proposed is to be open to ratification for all time."[100] Nor did the Supreme Court believe that

One of the staunchest advocates of the Equal Rights Amendment, Michigan congresswoman Martha W. Griffiths helped steer the amendment through both the House of Representatives and Senate in 1971. Although Griffiths passed away in 2003, many women's rights advocates still hold out hope that the amendment will one day be passed. Griffiths is pictured here in 1982 with governor-elect James Blanchard of Michigan.

"ratification in some of the states may be separated from that in others by many years and yet be effective."[101] Instead, the Court stated that under Article V of the Constitution, "proposal and ratification are not treated as unrelated acts, but as succeeding steps in a single endeavor, the natural inference being that they are not to be widely separated in time."[102] Thus, *Dillon v. Gloss* provides some answers, but it also raises some questions.

In *Coleman v. Miller* (1939), the Supreme Court again gave somewhat mixed signals. The court reiterated that Congress has the constitutional power to set reasonable time limits on ratification. The majority opinion found, however, that Congress alone could determine what constitutes a reasonable limitation. Because Congress can establish a deadline, some believe Congress can also review an amendment after receiving approval of three-fourths of the states. According to *Coleman v. Miller*, "the question whether the amendment had been adopted within a reasonable time would not be subject to review by the courts."[103] To supporters of the ERA, this means that Congress can also overlook the deadline placed upon ratification earlier. The Supreme Court also asserted that the merit of state ratifications was a "political question" in which "the ultimate authority" rests with Congress.[104] All of this means that the issue is still open for debate, and the ERA might still be added to the U.S. Constitution should the three-state strategy succeed.

Further, the text of the amendment itself did not contain the seven-year limitation, as did the Twentieth, Twenty-first, and Twenty-second amendments. Beginning with the Twenty-third Amendment, Congress still placed time limits on proposed amendments, but the wording was taken out of the text of the amendment. Such wording was instead inserted into congressional proposals. The Twenty-seventh Amendment, first proposed in 1789, is the exception to the post-Nineteenth Amendment time limitations imposed by Congress. In the cases in which the amendment included the deadline wording in the text, legal maneuvering does not matter: States that ratified such amendments gave approval to amendments that included a deadline. Such approval included a stipulated period for final ratification. Some believe that this alteration in practice allows Congress to determine whether the deadline matters. At the very least, the three-state strategy, if effective, would force Congress to examine the amendment for possible inclusion.

THE LEGACY OF THE WOMEN'S RIGHTS MOVEMENT

As for a constitutional amendment that guarantees equality, perhaps one of the greatest hurdles facing the ERA is that many of the goals of the amendment have already been realized through various decisions of the U.S. Supreme Court. Specifically, rulings on the equal protection clause of the Fourteenth Amendment and the Civil Rights Act of 1964 extended rights and protections to women—without the ERA. As one scholar put it, "There is no longer any question whether equality is constitutionally guaranteed to women. It is."[105]

At the same time, women made gains in professions formerly reserved for men. Although it has taken many years for women to realize some of the other measures of equality, such as equitable pay, many of these goals have been achieved. The courts consistently uphold women's rights to equality in this country, usually citing the protections in the Fourteenth Amendment, much as Susan B. Anthony and Francis and Virginia Minor argued in the 1870s. In short, the legal and cultural situation shifted without the ratification of the Equal Rights Amendment. Thus, much of the political energy has dissipated, because many of the issues originally addressed by the ERA have been adopted over the years.

Despite the obstacles, ERA supporters continue to support the amendment. The 1972 measure was introduced, debated, and passed in the Illinois House of Representatives in May 2003. The Illinois Senate failed to ratify the amendment

TITLE IX

In 1972, Congress enacted Title IX of the Education Amendments, usually referred simply as Title IX. The statute is only 37 words in length, and reads, "No person in the United States shall, on the basis of sex, be excluded from participation in, be denied the benefits of, or be subjected to discrimination under any education program or activity receiving Federal financial assistance."*

While the most visible and celebrated aspect of Title IX has been its effect on high-school and collegiate athletics, the law essentially deals with a host of educational activities and offerings. In reality, Title IX specifically deals with 10 different areas, only one of which is athletics. The other nine areas are "Access to Higher Education, Career Education, Education for Pregnant and Parenting Students, Employment, Learning Environment, Math and Science, Sexual Harassment, Standardized Testing, and Technology."** Each of these areas fall under federal oversight, because Congress funds these educational programs. Virtually no part of education is untouched by Title IX.

In 1979, the U.S. Department of Health, Education and Welfare (this cabinet department was separated the same year into the Department of Education and the Department of Health and Human Services) released a policy statement clarifying Title IX. This policy statement is now known as the *three-prong test*, which is used to judge an institution's compliance. The clarification stated that the three-prong

> test provides that an institution is in compliance if (1) the intercollegiate-level participation opportunities for male and female students at the institution are "substantially proportionate" to their respective full-time undergraduate enrollments, (2) the institution has a "history and continuing practice of program expansion"

before the legislative session ended the following year, however. In April 2005, the ERA won a majority vote in the Arkansas Senate (16–15, with 4 abstentions). Unfortunately,

For the underrepresented sex, or (3) the institution is "fully and effectively" accommodating the interests and abilities of the underrepresented sex.***

In other words, in order to ensure compliance, institutions need to address several issues. First, they must maintain relatively equal ratios of male/female opportunities, proportionate to the male/female ratios of their student enrollment. Second, they must demonstrate continual improvement and expansion of opportunities for the underrepresented sex (usually women). Finally, the institution should continue to provide additional opportunities for women.

Critics of Title IX charge that the law serves to harm male athletics. The law seeks to protect both genders, however, depending upon the situation. In fact, many lawsuits have been filed on behalf of men's opportunities in which Title IX is the legal basis for the claimants.

In October 2002, Congress renamed Title IX the Patsy T. Mink Equal Opportunity in Education Act, in honor of its primary author and former member of Congress, Patsy T. Mink (D-Hawaii), who died the previous month. The law is still commonly referred to by its better-known name of Title IX. The law continues to play an important role in promoting and maintaining equal educational opportunities for men and women.

---

* "A Policy Interpretation: Title IX and Intercollegiate Athletics." Available online at *http://www.ed.gov/about/offices/list/ocr/docs/t9interp.html*

** "Facts & Myths." Title IX. Available online at *http://www.titleix. info/content.jsp?content_KEY=179.*

*** "Further Clarification of Intercollegiate Athletics Policy Guidance Regarding Title IX Compliance." U.S. Department of Education. Available online at *http://www.ed.gov/about/offices/list/ocr/ title9guidanceFinal.html.*

Arkansas Senate rules require a majority of the total membership to ratify such measures. Thus, the measure failed to reach the necessary 18 votes.

In recent years, women have been elected and appointed to prominent positions in the federal government. In January 2007, California congresswoman Nancy Pelosi (pictured here) became the first female speaker of the House of Representatives, and former first lady Hillary Clinton is a two-term Senator from the state of New York and a presidential candidate for 2008.

Between 1923 and 1972, supporters managed to get the ERA introduced in each branch of Congress. Both the House and Senate finally passed the measure in 1972, and later extended the time limit to 1982. After failing to ensure ratification, supporters again began introducing the amendment in each session of Congress, an exercise that continues to this day.

Despite the failure of the ERA, women in the United States do enjoy equality with men. The women's rights movement of the nineteenth century forever changed the political process. The goals and ideals for which early leaders struggled to promote have been realized. Women voters now make up a majority of the American electorate, something that would no doubt delight Susan B. Anthony. Divorce rights, custody rights, and property rights now exist for women to a degree that would make Elizabeth Cady Stanton proud. Women are involved in politics to the point that they have won elections to virtually every office in the country. In January 2007, Nancy Pelosi, a member of Congress from California, became the first female Speaker of the House of Representatives. Although females have not held the positions of president and vice president, more and more female candidates are being mentioned and considered for those offices. Indeed, women have come a long way from the days in which their political opinion was neither desired nor tolerated. The early leaders did not live to see the day when women could stand on equal ground, but they helped pave the way. Their vision of female equality, if not complete, is still in process, and will continue to succeed. As Susan B. Anthony once declared, "Failure is impossible!"[106]

CHRONOLOGY

1608   First European women arrive at Jamestown,
                Virginia, a year after its founding.

1638   Massachusetts Bay Colony officials find Anne
                Hutchinson guilty of religious heresy and
                banish her from the colony.

1776   Abigail Adams appeals in vain for her husband,
                John, to "remember the ladies" in the new
                government.

1792   Mary Wollstonecraft's *A Vindication of the
                Rights of Women* is published.

Timeline

1869
The women's rights movement
splits into the radical National
Woman Suffrage Association
and the conservative American
Woman Suffrage Association

1920
Nineteenth
Amendment
gives women
the right to
vote

1848

1920

1848
First women's
rights convention
held in Seneca
Falls, New York,
where *Declaration
of Sentiments* is
adopted

1890
Wyoming
is the first
state to allow
women the
right to vote

1916
Jeannette Rankin
becomes the first
woman elected to
Congress

1833	Oberlin College, America's first coeducational college, is established; the Philadelphia Female Anti-Slavery Society is founded.
1837	Mary Lyons establishes the first women's college in the United States, Mount Holyoke Seminary.
1840	World Anti-Slavery Convention denies Lucretia Mott her seat because she is a woman.
1848	First women's rights convention is held in Seneca Falls, New York, and adopts the Declaration of Sentiments.
1849	Elizabeth Blackwell is the first woman to graduate from medical school in the United States.

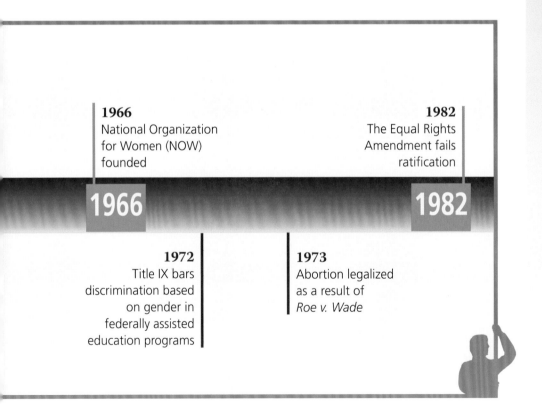

1966
National Organization for Women (NOW) founded

1982
The Equal Rights Amendment fails ratification

1966

1982

1972
Title IX bars discrimination based on gender in federally assisted education programs

1973
Abortion legalized as a result of *Roe v. Wade*

1866	The American Equal Rights Association is founded.
1869	The women's rights movement splits over the wording of the Fourteenth and Fifteenth amendments into the radical National Woman Suffrage Association and the conservative American Woman Suffrage Association; the Territory of Wyoming allows women to vote.
1872	Victoria Woodhull runs for president; Susan B. Anthony is one of several women who are fined for having voted in the presidential election.
1875	U.S. Supreme Court rules in *Minor v. Happersett* that citizenship does not guarantee the right to vote.
1878	The first Woman Suffrage Amendment is proposed in Congress.
1890	Wyoming enters the Union and is the first state to allow women the right to vote; National American Woman Suffrage Association is formed.
1893	Colorado amends its constitution to allow women the right to vote.
1895–96	Idaho and Utah amend their constitutions to allow women the right to vote.
1910	Washington State amends its constitution to allow women the right to vote.
1911	California amends its constitution to allow women the right to vote.
1913	Alice Paul leads a protest the day before President Woodrow Wilson's inauguration.
1916	Jeannette Rankin becomes the first woman elected to Congress.
1919	Congress passes the Nineteenth Amendment and sends it to the states for ratification.

1920	Women win right to vote with ratification of the Nineteenth Amendment; League of Women Voters is established.
1948	The United Nations adopts Universal Declaration of Human Rights.
1963	Betty Friedan publishes *The Feminine Mystique*.
1966	National Organization for Women (NOW) is founded.
1972	Title IX of the Education Amendments bars discrimination based on gender in federally assisted education programs.
1973	U.S. Supreme Court legalizes abortion in *Roe v. Wade*.
1981	Sandra Day O'Connor becomes the first woman to serve on the U.S. Supreme Court.
1982	The Equal Rights Amendment fails ratification.

NOTES

CHAPTER 1

1. The National American Woman Suffrage Association, *Victory, How Women Won It: A Centennial Symposium, 1840–1940* (New York: H.W. Wilson, 1940), 149.
2. Ibid., 151.
3. Ibid., 152.
4. Ibid.
5. Ibid.

CHAPTER 2

6. Eugene A. Hecker, *A Short History of Women's Rights.* Reprint (Westport, Conn.: Greenwood Press, Publishers, 1971), 13.
7. Ibid., 2.
8. Ibid., 23.
9. Ibid., 121.
10. Quoted in Ibid.
11. Ibid., 124–125.
12. Winston E. Langley and Vivian C. Fox, eds., *Women's Rights in the United States: A Documentary History* (Westport, Conn.: Greenwood Press, 1994), 1.
13. Quoted in Ibid., 21–22.
14. Quoted in Ibid., 22.
15. Quoted in Ibid.

CHAPTER 3

16. Christine A. Lunardini, *Women's Rights* (Phoenix, Ariz.: Oryx Press, 1996), 53.
17. "Lucretia Mott Quotes." About: Women's History. Available online at *http://womenshistory.about.com/od/quotes/a/lucretia_mott.htm*
18. Ibid.
19. *American Slavery as It Is: Testimony of a Thousand Witnesses*: Electronic Edition. Theodore D. Weld, Documenting the American South. Available online at *http://docsouth.unc.edu/neh/weld/weld.html.*
20. Hilda L. Smith and Berenice A. Carroll, eds., *Women's Political and Social Thought: An Anthology* (Bloomington: Indiana University Press, 2000), 182.
21. Miriam Sagan, *Women's Suffrage* (San Diego: Lucent Books, 1995), 14.
22. Ibid., 15.
23. Ibid.

CHAPTER 4

24. Elizabeth Cady Stanton, *Eighty Years and More: Reminiscences 1815–1897* (Boston: Northeastern University Press, 1993), 20.

138

25. Ibid., 21.

26. Elisabeth Griffith, *In Her Own Right: The Life of Elizabeth Cady Stanton* (New York: Oxford University Press, 1985), 10–11.

27. Stanton, *Eighty Years and More*, 43.

28. Lisa Frederiksen Bohannon, *Women's Rights and Nothing Less: The Story of Elizabeth Cady Stanton* (Greensboro, N.C.: Morgan Reynolds, 2001), 18.

29. Lois W. Banner, *Elizabeth Cady Stanton: A Radical for Woman's Rights* (Boston: Little, Brown, 1980), 19.

CHAPTER 5

30. Judith Wellman, *The Road to Seneca Falls: Elizabeth Cady Stanton and the First Woman's Rights Convention* (Urbana: University of Illinois Press, 2004), 183.

31. Quoted in Geoffrey C. Ward, *Not for Ourselves Alone: The Story of Elizabeth Cady Stanton and Susan B. Anthony* (New York: Alfred A. Knopf, 1999), 38.

32. Stanton, *Eighty Years and More*, 148.

33. Ward, *Not for Ourselves Alone*, 39.

34. Wellman, *The Road to Seneca Falls*, 198.

35. Quoted in Ward, *Not for Ourselves Alone*, 41.

36. Quoted in Wellman, *The Road to Seneca Falls*, 204.

37. Quoted in Ibid.

38. Quoted in Ward, *Not for Ourselves Alone*, 42.

39. Ward, *Not for Ourselves Alone*, 22.

40. Ibid.

41. Ibid., 23.

42. Ibid., 24.

43. Gerda Lerner, *The Grimké Sisters from South Carolina: Rebels Against Slavery* (Boston: Houghton Mifflin, 1967), 334.

44. Ward, *Not for Ourselves Alone*, 24.

CHAPTER 6

45. "Susan B. Anthony." Research.com. Available online at *http://www. reference.com/browse/wiki/ Susan_B._Anthony*

46. "Elizabeth Cady Stanton Dies at Her Home." *New York Times*, October 27, 1902 (obituary). Available online at *http://www. nytimes.com/learning/ general/onthisday/ bday/1112.html*

47. Ibid.

48. Famous Feminists. Available online at *http://www. depts.ttu.edu/wstudies/ WS43992006/famous_ feminists.htm*

49. Elizabeth Cady Stanton. Project Gutenberg eBook: *Eighty Years and More; Reminiscences 1815–1897.* Available online at *http:// www.gutenberg.org/ files/11982/11982-h/11982- h.htm*

50. Quoted in Griffith, *In Her Own Right*, 124.

51. Quoted in Ibid.

52. Quoted in Kathi Kern, *Mrs. Stanton's Bible* (Ithaca, N.Y.: Cornell University Press, 2001), 111.

53. Ibid., 110–111.

54. Philip S. Foner, ed., *Frederick Douglass: Selected Speeches and Writings*. The Library of Black America (Chicago, Ill.: Lawrence Hill Books, 1999), 600.

55. "Elizabeth Cady Stanton Dies at Her Home." *New York Times*, October 27, 1902 (obituary). Available online at *http://www. nytimes.com/learning/ general/onthisday/ bday/1112.html*

56. Ibid.

CHAPTER 7

57. United States Constitution Amendment XIV.

58. United States Constitution Amendment XV.

59. Quoted in Ward, *Not for Ourselves Alone*, 142.

60. Quoted in Lunardini, *Women's Rights*, 97.

61. *Minor v. Happersett*, 88 U.S. 162 (1874).

62. Ward, *Not for Ourselves Alone*, 142.

63. Ibid., 143.

64. Anonymous. The Project Gutenberg EBook: "An Account of the Proceedings on the Trial of Susan B. Anthony." Available online at *http://www.gutenberg. org/files/18281/18281- h/18281-h.htm*

65. Anonymous. The Project Gutenberg EBook: "An Account of the Proceedings on the Trial of Susan B. Anthony." Available online at *http://www.gutenberg. org/files/18281/18281- h/18281-h.htm*

66. "Sentencing in the Case of *United States vs Susan B. Anthony*." Available online at *http://www.law.umkc. edu/faculty/projects/ftrials/ anthony/sentencing.html*.

67. Ibid.

68. Ibid.

69. Ibid.

70. Ibid.

71. Ibid.

72. Ibid.

73. Ibid.

74. Elizabeth Cady Stanton, "Solitude of Self." *Not for Ourselves Alone*. Available online at *http://www. pbs.org/stantonanthony/ resources/index. html?body=solitude_self. html*

75. Quoted in Ward, *Not for Ourselves Alone*, 212.

76. Quoted in Ibid.

CHAPTER 8

77. Quoted in Jacqueline Van Voris, *Carrie Chapman Catt: A Public Life* (New York: Feminist Press, 1987), 5.

78. Kristina Dumbeck, *Leaders of Women's Suffrage* (San Diego: Lucent, 2001), 85.

79. Quoted in Van Voris, *Carrie Chapman Catt*, 12.

80. Carrie Chapman Catt and Nettie Rogers Shuler, *Woman Suffrage and Politics* (Seattle: University of Washington Press, 1969), 20.

81. Dumbeck, *Leaders of Women's Suffrage*, 93.

82. Ibid., 92.

83. Quoted in Van Voris, *Carrie Chapman Catt*, 140.

84. Eva Fan, "Nineteenth Amendment." Summer Skies: The Kent State Tragedy, Women's Rights in the Household, Work, and Education. Available online at *http://www.tqnyc.org/NYC063038/19amendment.htm*

85. "1878–1920: September 30, 1918—A Vote for Women." United States Senate. Available online at *http://www.senate.gov/artandhistory/history/minute/A_Vote_For_Women.htm*

86. "Women's Fight for the Vote: The Nineteenth Amendment." Exploring Constitutional Conflicts. Available online at *http://www.law.umkc.edu/faculty/projects/ftrials/conlaw/nineteentham.htm*

87. Ward, *Not for Ourselves Alone*, 224.

88. NAWSA, *Victory, How Women Won It*, 152.

CHAPTER 9

89. Gilbert Y. Steiner, *Constitutional Inequality: The Political Fortunes of the Equal Rights Amendment* (Washington, D.C.: The Brookings Institution, 1985), 61.

90. Whitney, 86.

91. Michael Barone, Grant Ujifusa and Douglas Matthews, *The Almanac of American Politics, 1972* (Boston: Gambit, 1972), 583.

92. Steiner, *Constitutional Inequality*, 66.

93. Quoted in Jane J. Mansbridge, *Why We Lost the ERA* (Chicago: University of Chicago Press, 1986), 66.

94. Barone, Ujifusa, and Matthews, *The Almanac of American Politics*, 739.

95. Steiner, *Constitutional Inequality*, 65.

96. Quoted in Ibid.

97. Republican Platform, 1980, *Congressional Quarterly Almanac*, 1980, 613.

CHAPTER 10

98. Allison Held, Sheryl Herndon, and Danielle Stager, "Why the ERA Remains Legally Viable and Properly Before the States," William and Mary Journal of Women and Law 3, no. 1 (spring 1997):1, 113–116.

99. "Legal Basis of the 'Three State Strategy.'"4ERA.

Available online at *http://www.4era.org/threestate.html*.

100. *Dillon v. Gloss*, 256 U.S. 368 (1921).

101. Ibid.

102. Ibid.

103. *Coleman v. Miller*, 307 U.S. 433 (1939).

104. Ibid.

105. Rex E. Lee, *A Lawyer Looks at the Equal Rights Amendment* (Provo, Utah: Brigham Young University Press, 1980), 83.

106. Quoted in Ward, *Not for Ourselves Alone*, 212.

BIBLIOGRAPHY

Banner, Lois W. *Elizabeth Cady Stanton: A Radical for Woman's Rights*. Boston: Little, Brown, 1980.

Barone, Michael, Grant Ujifusa, and Douglas Matthews. *The Almanac of American Politics, 1972*. Boston: Gambit, 1972.

———. *The Almanac of American Politics, 1974*. Boston: Gambit, 1974.

Bloomer, D. C. *Life and Writings of Amelia Bloomer*. New York: Schocken Books, 1975.

Bohannon, Lisa Frederiksen. *Women's Rights and Nothing Less: The Story of Elizabeth Cady Stanton*. Greensboro, N.C.: Morgan Reynolds, 2001.

Buechler, Steven M. *Women's Movements in the United States: Women Suffrage, Equal Rights, and Beyond*. New Brunswick, N.J.: Rutgers University Press, 1990.

Catt, Carrie Chapman, and Nettie Rogers Shuler. *Woman Suffrage and Politics*. Seattle: University of Washington Press, 1969.

Coleman v. Miller, 307 U.S. 433 (1939).

Congressional Quarterly Inc., ed. Republican Platform, 1980, *Congressional Quarterly Almanac*, 1980.

Cullen-DuPont, Kathryn. *The Encyclopedia of Women's History in America*. New York: Da Capo Press, 1998.

Dillon v. Gloss, 256 U.S. 368 (1921).

Dumbeck, Kristina. *Leaders of Women's Suffrage*. San Diego: Lucent, 2001.

Foner, Philip S., ed. *Frederick Douglass: Selected Speeches and Writings*. The Library of Black America. Chicago: Lawrence Hill Books, 1999.

Griffith, Elisabeth. *In Her Own Right: The Life of Elizabeth Cady Stanton*. New York: Oxford University Press, 1985.

Hecker, Eugene A. *A Short History of Women's Rights.* Reprint, Westport, Conn.: Greenwood Press, 1971.

Kendall, Martha E. *Failure Is Impossible! The History of American Women's Rights.* Minneapolis: Lerner, 2001.

Kern, Kathi. *Mrs. Stanton's Bible.* Ithaca, N.Y.: Cornell University Press, 2001.

Langley, Winston E., and Vivian C. Fox, eds. *Women's Rights in the United States: A Documentary History.* Westport, Conn.: Greenwood Press, 1994.

Lee, Rex E. *A Lawyer Looks at the Equal Rights Amendment.* Provo, Utah: Brigham Young University Press, 1980.

Lerner, Gerda. *The Grimké Sisters from South Carolina: Rebels Against Slavery.* Boston: Houghton Mifflin, 1967.

Lunardini, Christine A. *Women's Rights.* Phoenix, Ariz.: Oryx Press, 1996.

Mansbridge, Jane J. *Why We Lost the ERA.* Chicago: University of Chicago Press, 1986.

Matthews, Glenna. *American Women's History: A Student Companion.* New York: Oxford University Press, 2000.

Minor v. Happersett, 88 U.S. 162 (1874).

The National American Woman Suffrage Association. *Victory, How Women Won It: A Centennial Symposium, 1840–1940.* New York: H.W. Wilson, 1940.

Sagan, Miriam. *Women's Suffrage.* San Diego: Lucent, 1995.

Smith, Hilda L., and Berenice A. Carroll, eds. *Women's Political and Social Thought: An Anthology.* Bloomington: Indiana University Press, 2000.

Stanton, Elizabeth Cady. *Eighty Years and More: Reminiscences 1815–1897.* Boston: Northeastern University Press, 1993.

Steiner, Gilbert Y. *Constitutional Inequality: The Political Fortunes of the Equal Rights Amendment.* Washington, D.C.: The Brookings Institution, 1985.

Van Voris, Jacqueline. *Carrie Chapman Catt: A Public Life.* New York: Feminist Press, 1987.

Ward, Geoffrey C. *Not for Ourselves Alone: The Story of Elizabeth Cady Stanton and Susan B. Anthony.* New York: Alfred A. Knopf, 1999.

Wellman, Judith. *The Road to Seneca Falls: Elizabeth Cady Stanton and the First Woman's Rights Convention.* Urbana: University of Illinois Press, 2004

Whitney, Sharon. *Equal Rights Amendment: The History and the Movement.* New York: Franklin Watts, 1984.

FURTHER READING

Chafe, William H. *The Road to Equality: American Women Since 1962.* New York: Oxford University Press, 1994.

Eickhoff, Diane. *Revolutionary Heart: The Life of Clarina Nichols and the Pioneering Crusade for Women's Rights.* Kansas City: Quindaro Press, 2006.

Feeley, Dianne. *Why Women Need the Equal Rights Amendment.* New York: Pathfinder Press, 1973.

Feinberg, Renee. *The Equal Rights Amendment: An Annotated Bibliography of the Issues, 1976–1985.* New York: Greenwood Press, 1986.

Gleadle, Kathryn. *The Early Feminists: Radical Unitarians and the Emergence of the Women's Rights Movement, 1831–1851.* New York: St. Martin's Press, 1995.

Gustafson, Melanie Susan. *Women and the Republican Party, 1854–1924.* Urbana: University of Illinois Press, 2001.

Hatch, Orrin G. *The Equal Rights Amendment: Myths and Realities.* Irvine, Calif.: Savant Press, 1983.

Hurley, Jennifer A. *Women's Rights: Great Speeches in History.* San Diego: Greenhaven Press, 2002.

Ostrogorski, Moisei. *The Rights of Women: A Comparative Study in History and Legislation.* London: Swan Sonnenschein, 1893.

Peters, Julian, and Andrea Wolper, eds. *Women's Rights, Human Rights: International Feminist Perspectives.* New York: Routledge, 1995.

Roberts, Cokie. *Founding Mothers: The Women Who Raised Our Nation.* New York: William Morrow, 2004.

Schwarzenbach, Sibyl A., and Patricia Smith, eds. *Women and the U.S. Constitution: History, Interpretation, and Practice.* New York: Columbia University Press, 2003.

Stalcup, Brenda, ed. *The Women's Rights Movement: Opposing Viewpoints*. San Diego: Greenhaven Press, 1996.

Wolgast, Elizabeth H. *Equality and the Rights of Women*. Ithaca, N.Y.: Cornell University Press, 1980.

Wollstonecraft, Mary. *A Vindication of the Rights of Women*. Amherst, N.Y.: Prometheus Books, 1989.

WEB SITES

Famous Feminists
http://www.depts.ttu.edu/wstudies/WS43992006/famous_feminists.htm

American Slavery as It Is: Testimony of a Thousand Witnesses
http://docsouth.unc.edu/neh/weld/weld.html

A Policy Interpretation: Title IX and Intercollegiate Athletics
http://www.ed.gov/about/offices/list/ocr/docs/t9interp.html

Office for Civil Rights: Title IX
http://www.ed.gov/about/offices/list/ocr/title9guidanceFinal.html

Legal Basis of the Three-State Strategy
http://www.4era.org/threestate.html

An Account of the Proceedings on the Trial of Susan B. Anthony
http://www.gutenberg.org/files/18281/18281-h/18281-h.htm

Sentencing in the Case of *United States vs. Susan B. Anthony*
http://www.law.umkc.edu/faculty/projects/ftrials/anthony/sentencing.html

Women's Fight for the Vote: The Nineteenth Amendment
http://www.law.umkc.edu/faculty/projects/ftrials/conlaw/nineteentham.htm

Elizabeth Cady Stanton
http://www.nytimes.com/learning/general/onthisday/bday/1112.html

Revealing History: Strengthens the Major Parties
http://www.opendebates.org/theissue/strengthenmajorparties.html

"Solitude of Self.": Elizabeth Cady Stanton
http://www.pbs.org/stantonanthony/resources/index.html?body=solitude_self.html

Susan B. Anthony
http://www.reference.com/browse/wiki/Susan_B._Anthony

September 30, 1918: A Vote for Women
http://www.senate.gov/artandhistory/history/minute/A_Vote_For_Women.htm

Facts & Myths: Title IX
http://www.titleix.info/content.jsp?content_KEY=179

Nineteenth Amendment
http://www.tqnyc.org/NYC063038/19amendment.htm

Lucretia Mott Quotes
http://womenshistory.about.com/od/quotes/a/lucretia_mott.htm

PICTURE CREDITS

INDEX

ABOUT THE CONTRIBUTORS

Author **SHANE MOUNTJOY** resides in York, Nebraska, where he is associate professor of history and dean of students at York College. Professor Mountjoy holds degrees from York College, Lubbock Christian University, the University of Nebraska, and the University of Missouri. He and his wife, Vivian, home-school their four daughters—Macy, Karlie, Ainsley, and Tessa. Dr. Mountjoy has written several books on topics ranging from Spanish explorers to landmark Supreme Court decisions.

Series editor **TIM McNEESE** is associate professor of history at York College in York, Nebraska, where he is in his sixteenth year of college instruction. Professor McNeese earned an associate of arts degree from York College, a bachelor of arts in history and political science from Harding University, and a master of arts in history from Missouri State University. A prolific author of books for elementary, middle and high school, and college readers, McNeese has published more than 90 books and educational materials over the past 20 years, on everything from Picasso to landmark Supreme Court decisions. His writing has earned him a citation in the library reference work *Contemporary Authors*. In 2006, he appeared on the History Channel program *Risk Takers/History Makers: John Wesley Powell and the Grand Canyon*.